MAKING ADS PAY

by JOHN CAPLES

Vice President, Batten, Barton, Durstine & Osborn, Inc.
Author of "Tested Advertising Methods"
"Advertising for Immediate Sales," "Advertising Ideas"
Member, Guiding Faculty of The Famous Writers School

Dover Publications, Inc., New York

This Dover edition, first published in 1966, is an unabridged republication of the work originally published by Harper & Brothers Publishers in 1957.
This edition is published by special arrangement with Harper & Row, Publishers, Incorporated.

International Standard Book Number: 0-486-21575-X
Library of Congress Catalog Card Number: 66-17121

Manufactured in the United States of America
Dover Publications, Inc.
180 Varick Street
New York, N. Y. 10014

Contents

Foreword

By Paul B. West, former President,
Association of National Advertisers

John Caples' new book fills a serious void in the literature of advertising today.

As advertising has grown to its present status of a vital force in selling and profit, there seems to be a tendency even among the most competent authors to deal with an ever-increasing number of aspects of the advertising technique or approach such as motivation, pre-testing, post-testing, technological improvements, and a host of media selection methods and analyses. As excellent as these books are, and while they make valuable contributions to the specialized subjects they deal with, they also underscore the need for a book such as *Making Ads Pay* which deals with the basic fundamentals of advertising.

Much has been stated about advertising creativity—that elusive combination of experience, hard work, and imagination. Few would deny that John Caples is a creative man. In this book he has deftly managed to impart that creative touch by stressing the fundamentals of good copy but never strait-jacketing them with hackneyed formulas.

A number of the nation's leading companies today invest upwards of $50 million a year in their advertising. They know that advertising, or rather successful advertising, is essential not only to their continued growth but to their very existence. Therefore, to the students of advertising, to the many younger men and women new in advertising, and to those of us of longer experience in advertising, this book is a valuable guide to advertising fundamentals and how to apply them in order to achieve advertising productivity. After all, to all of us in advertising our main responsibility continues to be in *Making Ads Pay*.

1

Seven Steps to Successful Advertising

ONE BRIGHT Monday morning in September, a cub copy writer stood before the desk of the Copy Chief of a large New York advertising agency.

"Go to the proof files and get me a bunch of proofs of mail order ads. Bring them to my desk and I'll tell you which were successful in making sales and which were failures."

The speaker was Ev Grady, my new boss. He gave me my first job as an advertising writer.

Grady took the ad proofs which I handed to him and sorted them into two piles.

"These are the successful ads," he said, pointing to one pile. "Take these ads to your desk and study them. And study the failures too. Try to figure out what the successful ads have got that the failures haven't got. Then when you write your own ads, try to put into them the things that will make them successful."

That incident took place thirty-one years ago. I have been trying to follow Grady's advice ever since. It is good advice. *Test your ads. Then study the successes. Find out what the successes have got that the failures haven't got. Put into your new ads the qualities that will make them successful.*

This, in effect, is Darwin's theory of evolution applied to advertising. We all know that nature is continually experimenting with new types and new variations. Longer legs, shorter legs; bigger brains, smaller brains. The winning combinations are repeated, and the losers are discarded. Smart businessmen, politicians, actors, doctors, and scientists all follow this same principle. Experiment. Then repeat the winning combinations. Then improve on the winning combinations by means of further experimentation.

In thirty-one years I have studied the results of many advertising tests—mail order, opinion, readership, eye-camera, memory, sales area, split-run, impact, radio, television tests and a lot of others.

What makes a good advertisement? A few years ago, Keith Kimball, then a vice-president of BBDO, answered this question in the fewest and best words I ever heard:

A good advertisement is a believable promise to the right audience.

This definition applies to almost all types of advertising—newspaper, magazine, television, radio, and direct mail.

If you and I could follow the definition perfectly—if from now on we could learn to write nothing but believable promises to the right audience, we would not need to study the principles of advertising any further.

But the fact is, we need to know more than just a good definition. For example, a good definition of Christian ethics is "Do unto others as you would have others do unto you." If we could all follow that definition perfectly, we would not need to read the Bible.

But in the advertising business, as in our daily lives, we need something more specific than a definition. We need guidance in solving the problems that arise all the time.

"A good advertisement is a believable promise to the right audience." Some promises are more believable than others. Which are the most believable?

In writing an ad, you may have a number of believable

promises to choose from. Which promise should you feature in the headline or opening sentence? Which promise will be most effective in creating DESIRE?

Who is the right audience for your product or service and how do you go about attracting the right audience?

After you have attracted the right audience and induced them to believe your promises, how do you induce them to BUY NOW? This is important because if they postpone action, they may never act.

Advertising is simply *Selling*, multiplied by the printing press or by broadcasting. The advertising process can be broken down into a series of *steps*—step one, step two, etc. It is easier to take one step at a time than to take all the necessary steps at one leap.

Listed below are the seven basic steps in completing a sale by means of advertising. These are presented in the form of a series of questions or a check list. This check list is based on the results of hundreds of advertising tests. It is based on millions of dollars spent in experiments designed to find out what kind of advertising sells and what kind doesn't sell.

The next time you prepare an ad or a commercial, put this check list alongside of it. Make sure you have not forgotten to include the tested methods that make ads get action. You may not be able to include every method in every ad, but you should include all you can.

The Seven Basic Steps

1. *Does your ad attract the RIGHT AUDIENCE?*

The attention-getting device in a printed ad is the headline or the picture. In television it is the opening sentence of the commercial or the picture on the screen. In direct mail, it is the first sentence of the letter. Or perhaps a sentence printed on the envelope.

If your attention-getting device attempts to attract everybody by simply shouting, "Hey, everybody!" you may fail to attract the very people who might be induced to buy your product.

Here is a successful ad headline. It attracts the right audience for a mail order course in correct English:

"Do you make these mistakes in English?"

Warning: Do not inflate your readership or your listening audience by *attracting curiosity seekers* at the expense of *losing customers.*

2. *Does your ad HOLD the audience?*

Let us say that you have stopped a prospect with your headline or picture. But his finger is on the page (or on the TV dial). He is anxious to turn the page, and may do so immediately if you give him nothing but a selfish-sounding sales talk.

Sometimes subheads will hold the reader. Sometimes subillustrations. Frequently it is the first paragraph that holds him (or loses him). Here is the first paragraph of the successful ad mentioned above. Notice how it holds the reader *by continuing the same thought that was stated in the headline.*

DO YOU MAKE THESE MISTAKES IN ENGLISH?
Many persons use such expressions as "Leave them lay there" and "Mary was invited as well as myself." Still others say "Between you and I" instead of "Between you and me."

3. *Does your copy CREATE DESIRE?*

Does your copy promise plenty of benefits? Do you keep on piling up advantages, in short simple sentences? Do you drive home the chief advantages of your product by stating these advantages several times in different words?

4. *Do you prove it is a BARGAIN?*

Department stores do this by saying "Was $10 . . . now $5.95." Mail order book advertisers sometimes say: "Due to a purchase of a shipment of fine India paper, when prices were low, we are able to offer this volume at an extremely low price."

5. Do you establish CONFIDENCE?

After you have created desire and proved that the price is right, your prospect may say to himself: "I wonder if this is a gyp outfit? Maybe this gadget will break or bend or shrink or fall apart."

If you are writing advertising for a company such as General Electric or Du Pont, you do not have to worry much about establishing confidence. But if your client is not known to everybody, it is good to say things like: "Founded in 1898" . . . "Guaranteed by the U. S. Testing Laboratory" . . . "Money back if not delighted."

6. Do you make it EASY TO ACT?

Let us say you have done everything correctly up to now. You have stopped prospects and you have sold some of them on the idea of buying. Now is the time to make it *easy to act*. Mail order advertisers do this by including a coupon or an order blank. Some advertisers include telephone numbers and dealers' addresses. A manufacturer of typewriters increased his telephone orders by telling prospects just what to say on the telephone. The ad said:

Telephone this number and say "Please tell me how I can get a typewriter for 10¢ a day."

7. Do you give prospects a reason to ACT AT ONCE?

Perhaps you have successfully overcome all the preceding hurdles. Your prospect wants to act. He knows what the next step is. There is one last hurdle. It is inertia—the well-known human tendency to put it off. So include in your ad a reason to act NOW. For example: "Price going up" . . . "Supply limited" . . . "Shop early for best selections."

SUMMING UP

Here, briefly stated, are the seven basic action-getting devices. You can't use all of these in every ad, but it is good to use all you can.

1. Stop *prospects*.
2. *Hold* prospects.
3. Create *desire*.
4. Prove the *price* is right.
5. Prove it is *not a gyp*.
6. Make it *easy* to act.
7. Give the prospect a reason to *act now*.

Future chapters in this book explain tested ways to accomplish these objectives.

2

How I Wrote My First Advertisement

"YOUR FIRST assignment will be to write an advertisement for a book published by the Ralston University Press," said my boss, Ev Grady.

"The title of the book is 'The Cultivation of Personal Magnetism.' Write a full-page ad for *Physical Culture Magazine*. The ads in Physical Culture measure seven inches wide by ten inches high. There are three columns of copy—about 800 words—in each ad. You will need to write about 500 words. There are certain standard paragraphs which we include in every ad. It will not be necessary for you to rewrite these paragraphs. Just attach these standard paragraphs to your own copy."

"Ruth," said Grady turning to his secretary, "will you please give Mr. Caples an assignment slip for a full-page ad for Ralston University Press. Make it due—let me see, this is Monday—make it due Thursday."

In this conversation, Grady illustrated several principles of the advertising business.

1. Give a writer a definite *due date*. That is the way to make him *get going*.

2. Give a new writer time to get started. Grady gave me four days in which to write a single ad. Later on I was not given that much time.

3. It is not only permissible but also desirable to repeat in each

7

new ad certain standard, tested selling paragraphs that have been proved successful when tried out in previous ads.

"Now John," said Grady, "I'll tell you about this book. First let's look at some of those ad proofs you got from the files."

"Here is an ad we ran last summer in *Psychology Magazine*. It did pretty well." Grady picked up a proof. The picture showed a handsome man, smiling, and holding out his hand to shake hands.

The headline of the ad was printed in large type under the picture:

HIS VOICE—HIS MANNER—COMPEL YOU TO LISTEN

Alongside the picture was printed a subhead in boldfaced type. Grady read it aloud:

> You know him. He's the best salesman you ever met. He's the 'life of the party' wherever he goes. Men like him. Women like him. He is magnetic—irresistible. Listen to his voice: it's rich and vibrant. Watch his manner: it's confident and poised. People are attracted to him at once. They trust him. He is magnetic! And whether you are man or woman—you, too, can now acquire a magnetic voice—a magnetic personality.

I thought, "Gee, I wish I could be like that chap in the ad. I'm awkward in dealing with people. When I go to a party, I'm just a wallflower!"

"Here is some copy about the author of the book," said Grady, reading a selection from the middle of the ad:

> Edmund Shaftesbury and his great work need no introduction. The name of this extraordinary genius is linked with those of Gladstone, Queen Victoria, Lord Beaconsfield, Chief Justice Gray, Edwin Booth, Henry Ward Beecher. Such people as these, he helped to become powerful and

showed them how to release and use their personal magnetism. Quietly he taught his secrets to great thinkers, orators,
actors, statesmen, financiers, often receiving as much as $500
for a single course of private lessons! Many people found
new happiness, a new joy in living, through his teachings.
Now Edmund Shaftesbury's amazing teachings in personal
magnetism are available in book form—at the price of a
'best seller!'

"Here is the offer in the ad," said Grady, pointing to the
lower right-hand corner of the proof. He read aloud:

> Five days free examination. Just mail the coupon. Let me
> send you Edmund Shaftesbury's 'Cultivation of Personal
> Magnetism.' No money is necessary—all I ask is your name
> and address on the coupon. The volume will go forward to
> you at once.
> Read! Experience for yourself the surge of glorious new
> emotions! Discover your voice taking on a rich new quality!
> Experience the change from one personality to a magnetic
> new one! Within 5 days, if you aren't amazed and delighted,
> if you aren't inspired and impressed, repack the book and
> send it back to me without cost or obligation. Otherwise
> keep the book as your own and send only $3 in full payment
> for this great volume. You be the judge! Send off the
> coupon NOW.

I thought, "Maybe I'll send for the book!"
This was the first time I had been exposed to a hard-selling
mail order ad of the old school. It was making me want to buy
the product instead of wanting to write an ad about it!
The copy which Grady read to me illustrates several basic
principles of advertising that are worth remembering:

1. Write with *enthusiasm!*
2. Short, punchy sentences are effective.

3. Mention famous names if you can.

4. Start with a high price ($500 in this case) and work down to a low price.

5. Use a no-risk offer if you can.

"The appeal 'be popular' is a good one," said Grady. "We have used it on several different products and it has a lot of selling power. A lot of people are timid and self-conscious. They need something to bring them out and give them confidence. They need something to make them more effective in their business dealings and in their social life."

Grady picked up another ad proof and read the headline:

HAS THE SECRET OF PERSONAL MAGNETISM BEEN DISCOVERED AT LAST?

The ad was illustrated with a sketch of a jagged flash of lightning which ran diagonally down the page and pointed at the coupon.

"This ad pulled well," said Grady. "And pardon me, if I mention it," he added, with an apologetic laugh, "but I wrote it myself!

"Here is one we ran last January in the *Review of Reviews*. It did all right."

I read the headline: WHAT IS MAGNETIC ATTRACTION? The picture showed a photo of a young man sitting on a sofa with his arm around a girl. She had a blissful expression as if charmed by his personality.

I thought, "Gosh, if I read this book, maybe I'll be more successful with girls!"

Another ad had the headline, TRY THIS MILLIONAIRE'S SECRET OF SUCCESS FIVE DAYS FREE. This seemed appealing too.

Another had the headline, WHICH ONE HAS PERSONAL MAGNETISM? The picture showed a smiling, handsome chap at a social gathering. He was talking to a group of seven or eight men and women who were surrounding him and smiling admiringly at him. Sitting off in a corner by himself was a sad-faced guy who looked lonesome.

I thought, "That sad-looking guy is me!"

"One secret of writing good mail order copy is skillful exaggeration," said Grady.

He seemed a bit embarrassed to admit this business about exaggeration, but I admired his frankness. I thought, "I'm glad to be working for someone who will tell me the truth."

"But every product we advertise is sold with a *money back guarantee*," Grady hastened to add. "If the customer feels that we have overstated our case, he can get a refund right away and without any questions asked."

Is exaggeration justified? I once heard the following defense of it. See what you think.

All writers, including novelists, copy writers, and poets, are handicapped because they are able to put on paper only a small fraction of the emotion they feel inside of them. And when you, the reader, pick up a piece of writing, you are able to absorb only a small fraction of the emotion contained in the printed message. Therefore, the message which the writer tries to transfer from his brain to the reader's brain is twice diluted—first when the message is put on paper and second when the reader absorbs it from the paper.

When an author speaks to you via the printed page, he must shout in order to make you hear a whisper. He must weep copiously to make you shed a single tear. He must laugh uproariously to make you smile!

Compared with a house-to-house salesman, an ad writer is badly handicapped. The salesman can use tone of voice, facial expression, and gestures to drive his sales points home. He can watch the housewife's expression to see if his message is getting across. He can change his sales talk to fit different prospects.

And so, the handicapped copy writer, separated from his prospect by space and time, sometimes claims a lot in the hope that the reader will believe a little.

Exaggeration was not invented by ad men. The male pigeon puffs out his feathers in order to impress the female. The cat puffs up in order to frighten off a dog. A mother threatens a child with the bogey man. A political orator claims that the coming election is a contest between angels and devils. The police department says "Speed limit 25" hoping to keep you down to 35.

Ev Grady picked up one more of the ad proofs and said, "This ad is the most successful of all. We have repeated it a number of times. It sells more books than any of the others."

I studied the ad. Later on in my own office, I tried to imitate it. I was never able to write a personal magnetism ad that sold as many books as the champion ad. And so I was enormously impressed by the ad. It must *have something*.

I recently took from my file a proof of this ad. It seems to me it contains many of the success qualities learned from years of experience in mail order sales tests. Here is the headline:

GIVE ME 5 DAYS AND I'LL GIVE YOU
A MAGNETIC PERSONALITY
LET ME PROVE IT—FREE

"That chap who wrote the book looks very magnetic," I said pointing to the portrait of a distinguished-looking man in the ad.

"He didn't write the book," said Ev. "He is a model we picked up in Winemiller's studio. The author of the book didn't look magnetic enough to use in an ad."

I laughed and Ev laughed too. I felt that I was learning a lot on my first day.

"This ad is written in a style which we call the 'you and me' style," said Ev. "The author of the ad seems to be speaking directly to the reader in personal conversation. This style has been very effective in certain mail order propositions."

Since the headline of a mail order ad is the most important part of the ad, I think it will be instructive to analyze the above headline. Comments are in parenthesis.

GIVE ME 5 DAYS. (That is not asking for much. And it suggests that I'll get quick results. Best of all, I am not asked to spend money.)

I'LL GIVE YOU A MAGNETIC PERSONALITY. (What is this thing called a magnetic personality? It arouses my curiosity. Maybe it will make me popular. And I don't have to do any work. The man is going to give it to me.)

LET ME PROVE IT. (Good. I want to believe it. But I'm skeptical.)

"FREE" (The magic mail order word! It always attracts me. True, I've been fooled a few times, but maybe this time will be different. I think I'll read further. Maybe I can get something for nothing.)

And so the headline accomplishes its purpose. It gets me into the copy.

Below is the first part of the copy. Note the brief paragraphs— attractive to the eye, easy to read. Note that the copy is a continuation of the headline theme. One way to lose readers is to drop the headline theme when you get into the text.

I can so magnetize your personality that people will be drawn to you at once, irresistibly.

I can make you a magnet of human attraction so that you are popular everywhere, in any society.

I can show you how to use the amazing principle of magnetic control to win quick and conspicuous success in your business or profession.

I can place in your hands the key to supreme power and

happiness—give you a great new confidence in yourself—
overcome almost at once any timidity or self-consciousness
you may have.

I can give you a glorious new magnetic personality so that
you can influence the minds of others, attract people to
you instantly, be popular and well-liked wherever you go!

Let me prove it. Give me 5 days, and if in that time you do
not experience a new surge of personal power, if you do
not find yourself making friends wherever you may be, if
you do not discover yourself on the road to happiness,
wealth, and success—guided by my principles of personal
magnetism—the test will cost you nothing whatever. You
are the judge.

The above is 190 words of copy. The entire ad contains 800
words of copy. If this copy seems like over-statement, remember
that experience shows that mail order copy has to sell hard because:

1. A book of this kind is not a necessity. People do not have
to buy it as they do food and clothing. The desire for the book
has to be created.

2. *Mail order* copy has to do a complete selling job. It cannot
be simply reminder copy. It has to get attention, arouse interest, stimulate desire, and *get the order*—all with a single
printed page.

"As I mentioned before," said Grady, "We have found that
the appeal 'be popular' is a powerful appeal. It is something
that almost everybody wants.

"And another thing. People are lazy. They don't want to
work hard. They want a quick, easy way to solve their problems.
If you could hand the reader a pill and say 'Swallow this pill.
It will make you popular'—that would be the ideal thing. Re-

member that principle in writing ads. People want a quick easy way!"

I returned to my desk and went to work. I wrote an ad which Grady approved (after some editing), and which the client approved. The ad was tested in *Physical Culture Magazine* and did fairly well. It was run in a few other publications. During the next two years I wrote a number of other ads for the book on personal magnetism, but in all that time I was never able to write an ad that made as many sales as the ad with the photo of the distinguished-looking model and the magic headline:

GIVE ME 5 DAYS AND I'LL GIVE YOU
A MAGNETIC PERSONALITY
LET ME PROVE IT—FREE

3

How to Write Story Copy

"HERE IS an ad layout for Arthur Murray's mail order course in dancing," said Ev Grady one day.

He handed me a sheet of cardboard on which had been mounted an artist's drawing of an advertisement. The ad contained the following elements:

1. Picture. A pencil sketch of a dancing couple. The man and the girl both had black masks over their eyes and they were wearing fancy dress costumes. They were smiling and evidently having fun.

This picture was an effective "stopper." It made me wonder, "What is the romantic story behind the picture?"

In the years that followed, I was destined to learn these advertising principles:

(a) People are interested in *people*. Therefore pictures of people are among the best attention getters.

(b) If you show people in *unusual costumes*, the stopping power of the picture is often increased.

(c) If the artist does something unusual to a face, such as putting a black mask over the eyes, the attention value is further increased.

2. The ad layout which Grady handed me contained the following headline in large pencil letters:

HOW A FAUX PAS MADE ME POPULAR

I found this headline intriguing. The words "Faux Pas" had curiosity value. I wondered how the guy in the picture became popular by means of a "Faux Pas."

3. A subhead on the ad layout, in smaller letters than the headline, read as follows:

I never knew it was so easy to be popular until a humiliating experience showed me the secret.

4. The rest of the ad layout was blank white space except for a printed coupon which was pasted in the lower right-hand corner. This coupon copy is printed below. It is worth reading. Some day you may want to use a similar offer on your product or service.

Arthur Murray, Studio ooo
7 East 43 St., New York City.
Without obligating me in any way, please send me your Free Test Lesson and your beautifully illustrated 32-page book which tells all about Arthur Murray's course in dancing and explains how it can make me a graceful dancer right in my own home without music, partner or private teacher. I enclose 10¢ to cover postage and mailing.
Name _____
Address _____
City _____ State _____

Many advertisers have obtained the names and addresses of thousands of prospects by using offers of this kind. A booklet does not cost much to print and mail. Along with the booklet the advertiser can mail sales literature and an order blank.

The 10¢ which the prospect is required to send helps to weed out curiosity seekers who are not likely to buy the product.

Offers of booklets or samples of the product are appropriate in many advertising situations. These offers help sales in the long run. If you cannot make an immediate and complete sale with your ad, you should try to do the next best thing, namely, make a *partial* sale. Try to induce the prospect to take some simple, intermediate step which may eventually lead to a complete sale. Then follow up the prospect by mail or by a salesman's call. This technique will be explained more fully in a later chapter.

"What is the meaning of Studio 000?" I said, pointing at the address in the coupon.

"That's where the key number of the ad goes," said Grady. "When we send an ad to a publication, we also send a key number. The publication takes out the letters "ooo" and puts in the proper key number.

"Here is the key number in the coupon of this proof from *Physical Culture* magazine. It is Studio 99. That means that all the coupon replies addressed to Studio 99 will be credited to *that particular ad* in *that particular issue* of *Physical Culture*.

"Here is a proof from the October issue of *True Story*. You can see that the key number is Studio 262. Here is a proof from the October *Popular Mechanics*. The key number is Studio 503."

"Who keeps track of how many coupons each ad brings in?"

"Somebody over at Arthur Murray's office. The ads that bring a lot of coupons are repeated. Because they make money. The ads that don't pull are dropped. Because they lose money."

"What happens to ad writers whose ads don't pull?"

Grady laughed. "We advise them to go into some line of work which will be more suited to their talents," he said.

"Now what we want you to do is to write copy for this ad," continued Grady. "You are to fill the white space in this ad layout with a story that will fit the headline 'How a Faux Pas Made

Me Popular.' You can study old ad proofs and read some of the stories that we have run before."

I listened intently because I liked the advertising business and wanted to stay in it. My favorite subjects at school had been writing and drawing. Advertising seemed to be a combination of writing and drawing. What a delightful way to earn a living!

"Now I'll tell you about this headline for Arthur Murray's course," said Grady. "We have hopes it will do well because it is similar to some previous headlines of successful ads. We had an ad for a course in real estate selling which outpulled all the other real estate ads. The headline was: HOW A FOOL STUNT MADE ME A STAR SALESMAN.

"We had a very successful ad for a course of treatments that helped men grow new hair. The headline was: HOW A STRANGE ACCIDENT SAVED ME FROM BALDNESS.

"You can see the same idea running through all these headlines. Each one contains some *curiosity words* such as 'fool stunt,' 'faux pas,' or 'strange accident.' And each headline contains a reward such as 'made me a star salesman,' 'saved me from baldness,' or 'made me popular.' "

Note to reader: I hope you will give particular attention to what Grady said because it is *valuable advice!* He was describing a formula which worked 31 years ago and which I feel sure will work 31 years from today. And I expect it will work 310 years from today. This formula is based on human nature and human nature does not change. It took millions of years to build human nature into what it is today, and a period of a few years added to millions of years is not going to make much difference. Grady's formula can be summed up in two words, namely, "Curiosity. . . . Reward." Remember that formula and use it. Styles in advertising may change, but not the basic principles. The earliest ads were posters offering rewards for the return of lost slaves. Then handbills came into style. Then newspaper ads. Then magazines, direct mail, radio, television. Styles and techniques may change but the people you are trying to reach do not change. These people have the human trait of *curiosity*. And they want *rewards*. "Curiosity. . . . Reward." Use that formula. It works! I used it a few weeks ago in an advertisement for one of our client's products and the ad brought excellent sales results.

As mentioned before, this business of reworking old successful elements into new successes is not peculiar to the advertising business. It works in other types of business. It works in engineering. It works in medicine. It works in life. It is a basic principle.

Some writers and artists say that formulas are bad—that the reworking of old successes tends to hamper creative imagination and gets your mind into a rut. All right, discard the tested formulas if you want to. Go back to the stone age! Throw away your tools and go into the woods and start catching birds with your bare hands and digging for edible roots with your fingernails!

Actually, the reworking of old successes gives your imagination a higher platform to spring from. Add your own imaginative touch. And at regular intervals try something utterly new and different. But don't forget to rework old successes.

I went to my desk and studied proofs of old ads for Arthur Murray's course. I found it was possible to classify the ads into two types: (1) straight selling ads, and (2) story ads.

The headlines of these ads are worth studying because they contain much of the essence of selling that was learned in the hard school of mail order advertising where advertising has to pay its way in actual, traceable sales.

Here are typical headlines of the straight selling ads. All of the ads were illustrated by photographs of people dancing.

NEW STEPS FOR OLD—THE ARTHUR MURRAY WAY

CAN YOU DO THIS EASY STEP? THEN I CAN MAKE
YOU A GOOD DANCER IN 10 DAYS . . .
BY ARTHUR MURRAY

NEW WAY TO BE POPULAR—QUICKLY

DON'T BE A WALLFLOWER!
(Subhead) SEE HOW EASILY YOU CAN BECOME A GOOD DANCER—
THIS NEW WAY!

Here are typical headlines of the story ads:

HOW I ACQUIRED POISE AND POPULARITY.

HOW I BECAME POPULAR OVERNIGHT.

HOW I WAS SHAMED INTO POPULARITY.

Apparently both kinds of headlines had worked successfully because so many of both kinds had been used. However it was my job to write a *story ad* and so I went to work.

First I read the stories in the story ads. Here is how one of them started off:

HOW I BECAME POPULAR OVERNIGHT
They used to avoid me when I asked for a dance. Some said they were tired. Others had previous engagements. Even the poorest dancers preferred to sit against the wall rather than dance with me. But I didn't "wake up" until a partner left me standing alone in the middle of the floor.

What kind of a story could I write that would fit the "Faux Pas" headline? For a while, my mind played around with a remark a friend had made about a "faux pas." I recalled enough of my French lessons at school to know that "faux" means "false" and "pas" means "step." Years ago there were popular dance steps called the "one step" and the "two step." This friend of mine liked to show off his knowledge of French and so in conversation he sometimes referred to these two dance steps as the "un pas" (one step) and the "deux pas" (two step). One time this chap attended a dance and afterwards I asked him how it went. He replied with a laugh, "There was nothing but un pas, deux pas, and faux pas!"

I wondered if I could work this remark into an ad. Somehow it didn't seem to fit. So I dropped it.

Then my mind switched to another experience. I recalled a summer vacation when I was sixteen years old and I was made unhappy because I was unable to dance.

I spent a week at a summer boarding house with fellows and girls. During the day while we were swimming and canoeing I was as popular with the girls as any of the fellows. But at night when the phonograph was turned on and the young people danced on the porch, I was ignored by the girls because I didn't know how to dance. I sat sadly on the sidelines—a wallflower.

And so, years later, as a copy writer I decided to write the story of how a wallflower became a wildflower in a few easy lessons. Here is the story. To save your time, I have briefed it.

HOW A FAUX PAS MADE ME POPULAR

The day I met Grace, we went swimming. There was another chap along—Harry something—a dapper, grinning fellow with his hair slicked back. I didn't see how Grace could stand him.

That night at the hotel dance, I learned a lesson. Grace and Harry saw me standing on the sidelines and came toward me.

"Aren't you going to ask me to dance?" Grace called gaily, as the music started.

I flushed, realizing I couldn't dance a step. "Why I'd love to, but—I can't Tango!"

"That's a waltz!" Grace laughed.

"I don't waltz either," I faltered, realizing I had made a faux pas—a blunder.

"I don't think you want to dance with me at all!" she flashed.

Before I could explain further, she and Harry, a wonderful dancer, had glided away. I fled in disgrace.

The above incident satisfied *part* of the requirement of the headline, namely, it mentioned the words "faux pas."

Now I had to add some copy that would satisfy the rest of the headline, namely, how I became popular. Here it is:

That night I realized that I could never be popular unless I learned to dance. I had heard of a new way to learn—at home, without music or teacher. Arthur Murray, America's foremost dancing instructor, had perfected this method. I sent for his free booklet and test lesson.

The booklet and test lesson arrived promptly. I was amazed at the ease with which I was able to master the steps.

At this point I realized that I would also have to explain the masks on the dancing couple in the ad illustration and so I wrote the following:

I continued learning, so that I could attend the coming mask ball at the hotel.

THAT EXCITING NIGHT

What an exciting night that was! I danced with many partners, keeping perfect time, gliding around like a professional!

At this point I thought of a story twist which I think would have pleased my instructor whose course in short story writing I had previously taken at Columbia. And so I wrote:

Midnight found me dancing with a charming creature in a soft clinging costume.

"Where did you learn to dance so divinely?" she murmured. She was masked, but her voice thrilled me strangely. Later I told her how I had met and lost a beautiful girl—how wretched I felt—how I learned to dance in my room.

She caught my hand. "Oh, I'm so sorry—" Her voice broke—the voice that thrilled so strangely.

I brushed aside her mask. Imagine my wonder—surprise —joy! It was Grace smiling up at me!

What wonderful times we had after that!—parties—balls— dances. The day I wrote to Arthur Murray was the luckiest in my life.

At this point I added to my copy the standard closing paragraphs clipped from a previous ad, as follows:

This story is typical. Thousands have learned to dance quickly and easily through Arthur Murray's course. And so can you.

FREE . . . 32-PAGE BOOKLET AND TEST LESSON Read Mr. Murray's 32-page illustrated booklet and try the free test lesson which proves how easy it is to learn. The book tells how Mr. Murray became private instructor to the "400" and how he taught over 250,000 people to dance by mail.

"That's a swell ad! We will test it in the *New York Daily News*," said Ev Grady.

One morning Ev said, "Your ad is in the *News* today."

I immediately left the office and went to the nearest news-stand. The ad looked wonderful. It was my first ad in print and the second ad I had ever written in my life. (My first ad on personal magnetism was written for a monthly magazine and had not yet appeared.)

I stood on the street corner near the newsstand, reading my immortal words in a daily newspaper. I was oblivious to the traffic noises and people bumping into me. I felt almost as happy as the day I saw my first poem printed in a college magazine. Not long after that, my salary was raised from $25 to $30 a week.

I previously mentioned taking a course in short story writing at Columbia. Well, I never did get a story accepted by a national magazine. But I did write a lot of ad stories that have run in a number of publications. So the short story course at Columbia paid off, but in a different direction than originally intended.

SUMMING UP

1. One of the most effective ways to sell an idea is by telling a story. This technique began as far back as the Parables in the Bible and the fables of Aesop.

2. If you can't make a complete sale with an ad, try to make a partial sale. Offer a sample or a booklet.

3. Remember Ev Grady's formula. Arouse curiosity. Offer a reward.

4

They Laughed When I Sat Down
at the Piano

HERE IS a paragraph from a humorous article on advertising which appeared in *The New Yorker* magazine. I quote this item because I want to answer a question which the author of the article asked.

> After seeing a film about advertising men, we decided to have a talk with an advertising man we have long heard about, Mr. John Caples, a vice president of Batten, Barton, Durstine & Osborn, and a man who did as much as Calvin Coolidge to contribute to the merriment of the middle twenties. Who does not remember his "They Laughed When I sat Down at the Piano—But When I Started to Play!" or his "They Grinned When the Waiter Spoke to Me in French—But Their Laughter Changed to Amazement at My Reply!"? Mr. Caples put these together when he was only twenty-five and could barely make his way through either "Chopsticks" or a French menu. We asked him how his inspiration came to him, and found him as inarticulate as a poet on that score.

I recall that a writer from *The New Yorker* did ask how the ads came to be written and I was unable to answer. But that doesn't mean that there wasn't any answer. I was taken unawares by the question. Nobody had asked that question before and I was unable to put the answer into words on short notice. If the writer had taken me to a nearby bar and we had had a few drinks and chatted in a leisurely manner for an hour or so, I might have been able to answer his question.

As a matter of fact this question of how ideas are born has been asked frequently in recent years, and many of the answers have been vague. If the question could be answered clearly and definitely, it might be a helpful thing because it might point the way toward originating more and better ideas in the future.

I propose to answer the question in regard to one specific ad, namely, "They Laughed When I Sat Down at the Piano." I believe I can do this, because I have thought about the question from time to time, ever since that writer asked it, and because I have before me my advertising files from 31 years ago.

The first step toward the writing of this ad was the stimulus that got me started. Here it is:

"John, I wish you would get up an ad for the U.S. School of Music," said Ev Grady one day. "Write some headlines first, and we will go over them together."

That was the original stimulus—a *definite assignment*. It was my job to write ads. I had to write or get fired. It was economic necessity. A farmer summed up economic necessity when he said to one of his hogs in the barnyard, "Root, hog, or die!"

Grady gave me a due date which was typed on an assignment slip. That is another aid to creative thinking—a due date when the job must be finished. That helps to overcome procrastination and inertia, those drag-you-down forces which keep so many enterprises from being completed.

Grady gave me an easy way to start. He said, "Write some headlines first and we will go over them." That enabled me to take a small bite of the assignment and chew on it before tackling the major portion.

I started on this job as I had been trained to do on previous assignments, namely, I started with *research*. I started by looking at proofs of previous ads. Here are some of the headlines:

BE YOUR OWN MUSIC TEACHER—LEARN AT HOME

LEARN TO PLAY IN "DOUBLE QUICK TIME"—
THIS NEW EASY WAY

PLAY JAZZ ON THE "SAX"

I WAS AFRAID OF THIS NEW WAY TO LEARN
MUSIC—UNTIL I FOUND IT WAS EASY AS A-B-C

THEY THOUGHT I WAS BLUFFING WHEN I
TOLD THEM I LEARNED MUSIC WITHOUT
A TEACHER

DON'T ALWAYS BE A LISTENER . . . HAVE PART
IN THE FUN YOURSELF

IT SEEMED SO STRANGE TO HEAR HER PLAY

I spent several hours studying these ads, reading the copy and jotting down headline ideas of my own. After awhile I typed eight headlines on a sheet of paper and handed them to Ev Grady. Here they are:

THEY LAUGHED WHEN I SAT DOWN
AT THE PIANO—
BUT WHEN I STARTED TO PLAY!

MY FRIENDS LAUGHED AT THIS NEW WAY
TO LEARN MUSIC—
BUT NOW THEY BEG ME TO PLAY!

I COULDN'T BELIEVE IT WAS MY WIFE PLAY-
ING THE PIANO UNTIL I SAW WITH MY OWN
EYES

CAN YOU PLAY THE PIANO?
NEITHER COULD I THREE MONTHS AGO

I NEVER EVEN SAW MY MUSIC TEACHER
BUT HE TAUGHT ME TO PLAY JUST THE SAME

I COULDN'T BELIEVE MY EARS—
MARY HAD ACTUALLY LEARNED MUSIC
WITHOUT A TEACHER

GIVE ME 10 MINUTES AND I'LL PROVE
YOU CAN LEARN MUSIC WITHOUT A TEACHER

"WHAT A WAY TO LEARN MUSIC!" THEY LAUGHED
NOW MY FRIENDS BEG ME TO PLAY

Grady spent a minute or two looking at the headlines and
then he checked with a pencil the first headline on the list—
the one that begins with the words, "They laughed." "Write
copy to go with that headline," he said.

Regarding the headline he checked, I want to make an ob-
servation. I based the headline on a previously successful headline, "It seemed so strange to hear her play." This ad told the
story of a woman who visited the home of a girl friend. During
the visit the girl friend played the piano and the woman visitor
said in effect: "It seemed so strange to hear her play, because
I never knew before that she could play the piano."

I thought, "If that ad was successful, why wouldn't it be even
more effective to carry the idea further—to have a larger audience
—to have a chap laughed at by his friends when he made
believe he could play the piano, and then have him amaze his
friends by playing wonderfully well?

The point I want to make is that my headline was simply a
projection—a carrying further of a previously successful idea.
This is important. Few new ideas are born all at once (unless

they are stumbled on by accident). Most successful ideas are simply a carrying further of some previously successful idea. The proper technique is to study the failures and study the successes and discover in which *direction* you should travel to increase results. If you are a bird searching for a warmer climate and you fail to find it by flying north or east or west, you should then fly south.

Here is how the copy started. It was a story headline that Grady had checked and therefore I had to write a story.

THEY LAUGHED WHEN I SAT DOWN
AT THE PIANO
BUT WHEN I STARTED TO PLAY!

Arthur had just played "The Rosary." The room rang with applause. I decided that this would be a dramatic moment to make my debut. To the amazement of all my friends, I strode confidently over to the piano and sat down.

Question: Why did I select the Rosary as the piece for Arthur to play? It was not a particularly appropriate piece for entertaining a party of young merry makers. Do you recall the words that go with the music?

The hours I spent with thee, dear heart
Are as a string of pearls to me.
I count them over, every one apart
My rosary, my rosary!

Later in the song these words occur:
Oh memories that bless and burn!
Oh barren gain and bitter loss!

Now these words, and the haunting melody that accompanies them, are not the sort of thing that sets girls to giggling and fellows to doing parlor tricks.

Why did I choose to have Arthur play "The Rosary"? Now

that I look back on it, it seems to be an inappropriate selection.

The reason I chose it was because it was the only piece I could think of at the time. And why was it the only piece I could think of? Because ever since my childhood days my father had played that piece on the piano. Many evenings when he returned home from his office, he played it. It used to relax him to play the piano after a hectic day. Mother and I used to sit and listen to him play. Usually mother left the lights turned off, even when it began to get dark. She said that he played better that way. And you could listen better that way too. As the twilight deepened, you could sit and listen to the music and dream with your eyes wide open.

Father played well. And with emotion! I never learned to play the piano, but father played well enough for both of us. He used to play many pieces, but the one I remember best is "The Rosary." "The hours I spent with thee, dear heart!" You would imagine that I would think of some youthful romance as I write those lines. But I don't. I think of my father playing the piano in our home many years ago.

The reason I go into detail on this is simply to point out that even though I never learned to play the piano, I have a feeling and affection for piano playing that helped me in writing piano copy.

Now to get back to the story in the ad. It was necessary to set the stage for the chap who was going to amaze his friends. And so I wrote:

> "Jack is up to his old tricks," somebody chuckled. The crowd laughed. They were all certain I couldn't play a single note.
>
> "Can he really play?" I heard a girl whisper to Arthur.
>
> "Heavens no!" Arthur exclaimed. "He never played a note in all his life . . . But just you watch him. This is going to be good."

I decided to make the most of the situation. With mock

dignity, I drew out a silk handkerchief and lightly dusted off the piano keys. Then I rose and gave the piano stool a quarter of a turn. Just as I had seen an imitator of Paderewski do in a vaudeville sketch.

Note: Years before that, I had seen just such a sketch on the stage—the sort of clowning which Victor Borge does today before he plays the piano.

I decided to end the first portion of the copy with a joke I had read in a magazine. Here it is:

"What do you think of his execution?" called a voice from the rear.

"We're in favor of it!" came back the answer, and the crowd rocked with laughter.

Now the scene is all set and ready for a change of pace. We have created a scene of laughter and derision and it must be changed to admiration and amazement. No more time for kidding. It is time for Jack to get down to serious business.

Now I want to tell you how I was aided in writing about Jack's triumph by a piece of piano copy which I had read in a textbook entitled "Advertising Copy" by George Burton Hotchkiss. It was an emotional piece of copy and it stirred me up. As I mentioned before, laughter begets laughter and emotion begets emotion. A famous Greek playwright said: "If you want me to laugh, you must laugh first. If you want me to weep, you must weep first."

I recall an experiment by a physics professor at Columbia. He fastened two metal tuning forks beside each other on the desk. He struck one fork a hard blow with a hammer. Its music rang through the classroom like the sound of a gong. Then the professor seized the vibrating fork with his hand and its music stopped. But lo and behold, the other tuning fork had started to vibrate and was giving off the same musical note! It had been caused to vibrate by invisible waves, travelling from one tuning fork to the other!

Emotional vibrations work the same way. They travel from one person to another. They are contagious. "If you want me to laugh, you must laugh first. If you want me to weep, you must weep first." Don't forget that rule when you write advertising copy.

I would like to quote here and now the piano ad from the Hotchkiss textbook. I want you to judge for yourself whether or not it is emotional. I want you to see how this copy led logically and naturally to the piano copy which I wrote. I want you to see how the reading of emotional copy can stimulate a writer to create his own emotional copy. When you have seen this method at work, you can use the same method to stimulate your own writing.

The piano ad I am going to quote is long, but it is good copy and I hope you will read it clear through. Here is how Hotchkiss introduces it:

> Legends of famous musical classics like Beethoven's Moonlight Sonata and Liszt's Second Hungarian Rhapsody have been beautifully told in advertisements of the Duo-Art piano. The following is a fine example of its kind:

THE STORY OF A WINTRY NIGHT
ONE HUNDRED YEARS AGO

For those who know, and those who have yet to know, the soul-soothing beauty of Beethoven's "Moonlight Sonata"

Cold brilliant moonlight silvered the snowy roofs of quaint old Bonn. Through a narrow street the master was walking with a friend. "Hush!" he exclaimed, halting suddenly in front of a little house. "Listen! That is my Sonata in F. How well it is played!"

They edged up close to the door. In the midst of the finale the music ceased abruptly, and a voice cried sadly, "I can't play any more. It is so beautiful. Oh, if only I might go to Koln to the concert! If only I might hear it played by the master!"

"Yes, sister, but why wish for what cannot be?" said a second voice . . .

"Let us go in," said Beethoven. And, despite his friend's objection, he placed his hand on the latch. "I shall play for her and she will understand."

THE MASTER ENTERS

He opened the door. There at the table sat the brother mending shoes. The girl, crying softly, bowed her head upon the old piano.

"Pardon me, but I heard your music," said Beethoven, "and I also heard your wish. Perhaps, if you will allow me, I can fulfill it."

The cobbler thanked him. "But our piano is so poor," he apologized, "and we have no music."

"No music?" exclaimed the master, "how then does she . . . Oh, forgive me!" he stammered. The girl had lifted her head and he saw that she was blind . . .

She gave Beethoven her place at the piano. He ran his fingers along the yellowed keys. Under his touch the worn strings sang as if born anew, and out of the old instrument trooped hosts of his compelling melodies to surround and captivate the wondering pair. The flame of the one candle sputtered fitfully, and presently went out. The youth slipped over and threw open the shutters. As the moonlight flooded the room, the pianist paused.

"Who and what are you?" gasped the cobbler, scarce knowing he was speaking.

"Listen," answered the master, and he played the first few
bars of his Sonata in F.

"Beethoven!" burst from the lips of the pair. "Oh, play on,
play on—just a little more!" they pleaded as he arose to go.

THE MASTERPIECE IS CREATED

For a moment he stood, silent, looking out the window.
And then again seating himself, he began as if to voice the
spirit of the calm, perfect night, weaving slowly into exquisite being those mystic measures which caress the soul,
even as the cool radiance of the moon softens and gentles
the world's rough face. There, in that little room, Beethoven intertwined the throbbing of the sea's great heart and
the far, clear call of the stars; he sounded the very depths
of the sublime, till it seemed to the three listeners as if the
Spirit of Infinity were come down the path of moonlight
and stood by their side, whispering of the things that are
forever and forever.

Vain yearnings and thoughts of toil and tithes were swept
from their long-time moorings in the mind, and by the
hand of infinite loveliness, the blind girl was guided to
heights whence she saw more than wide eyes can window,
however clear . . .

Beethoven, the master, had in that hour, in that poor,
trouble-shadowed home, lighted a transforming flame which
would neither waver nor go out through all the years.

With this story in the back of my head, I wrote my own
copy. You will recall that we left Jack sitting on a piano stool.
The crowd had just laughed at his clowning. They had said

they were in favor of his "execution." Now it is up to Jack to do an about face and amaze the audience. I began the second portion of the ad with a subhead.

THEN I STARTED TO PLAY

Instantly a tense silence fell on the guests. The laughter died on their lips as if by magic. I played through the first few bars of Beethoven's immortal Moonlight Sonata. I heard gasps of amazement. My friends sat breathless—spellbound!

I played on and as I played I forgot the people around me. I forgot the hour, the place, the breathless listeners. The little world I lived in seemed to fade—seemed to grow dim—unreal. Only the music was real. Only the music and the visions it brought me. Visions as beautiful and as changing as the wind-blown clouds that long ago inspired the master composer. It seemed as if the master musician himself were speaking to me—speaking through the medium of music—not in words but in chords. Not in sentences but in exquisite melodies!

I typed my copy neatly and took it to Grady.

"That's swell!" he said. "It has real feeling. But something is missing."

"What's missing?"

"You should have Jack's friends congratulate him on his wonderful playing. And then Jack should tell how he took the U.S. School of Music course."

I returned to my desk and wrote the following:

A COMPLETE TRIUMPH!

As the last notes of the Moonlight Sonata died away, the room resounded with a sudden roar of applause. I found myself surrounded by excited faces. How my friends carried on! Men shook my hand—wildly congratulated me—pounded me on the back in their enthusiasm! Everybody was exclaiming with delight—plying me with rapid questions . . .

"Jack! Why didn't you tell us you could play like that?" . . . "Where did you learn?" . . . "How long have you studied?" . . . "Who was your teacher?"

"I have never even seen my teacher," I replied. "And just a short while ago I couldn't play a note."

"Quit your kidding," laughed Arthur, himself an accomplished pianist. "You've been studying for years. I can tell."

"I have been studying only a short while," I insisted. "I kept it a secret so I could surprise you."

Then I told them the whole story.

"Have you heard of the U.S. School of Music?" I asked. A few of my friends nodded. "That's a correspondence school, isn't it?" they exclaimed.

"Exactly," I replied. "They have a new simplified method that can teach you to play by mail in just a few months."

I have quoted the first three sections of the U.S. School of Music ad, namely,

1. The clowning scene
2. The playing of the Moonlight Sonata
3. The congratulation scene

The ad contained four additional sections as follows:

1. Subhead: How I Learned to Play Without a Teacher
   (4 paragraphs of copy)
2. Subhead: Play Any Instrument
   (1 paragraph of copy)

3. Subhead: Send for Our Free Booklet and Demonstration Lesson

(2 paragraphs of copy)

4. Coupon

The reason for such long copy is because mail order advertisers have found that they can get more sales with long copy than with short copy.

When this ad was typed, it occupied four typewritten pages, single spaced. The copy was given to the art department where it was illustrated with a picture of Jack at the piano, surrounded by his friends.

The ad was tested in *Physical Culture* magazine in December 1925. During the next few years it was run in a long list of magazines and newspapers. In some publications it was repeated a number of times. I do not have the sales records on the ad, but it was the best or one of the best that the U.S. School of Music ever ran. The ad was reproduced years later in a book by Julian Watkins entitled "The 100 Greatest Advertisements."

SUMMING UP

Here are some aids to creative copy writing, based on the above experience:

1. A specific assignment.

2. A due date.

3. Research. Study past successes. Determine in which direction success lies and go in that direction.

4. Start by writing headlines.

5. In addition to facts, get EMOTION into your copy. Your own emotion. Or somebody else's.

6. Find a good critic—a good copy chief to inspire and guide you.

5

They Grinned When the Waiter Spoke to Me in French

THE PREVIOUS chapter showed how it is possible to produce a successful ad by combining experience, research, emotion, constructive criticism, and the guidance of a good copy chief.

Now I want to point out that when a successful formula has been created, it can be used to solve other problems besides the original problem.

Many idea men (and women) such as writers and artists and inventors are not interested in formulas. They do not care to paint the same picture twice. Once a formula has been discovered and tested, they discard it and start in a new direction.

That is fine. That is the way it should be. That leads to the discovery of new formulas, either by design (as atomic energy was discovered) or by accident (as penicillin was discovered).

But the business man is different from the idea man. The business man wants to make money. *He has to make money* in order to stay in business. If he can make money by discovering a new formula, he is happy. If he can make money by repeating an old formula, he is just as happy.

All life and progress are an endless repetition of two basic urges. Repeat the successful. Try something new. Repeat the successful. Try something new. The business man. The idea man. The business man. The idea man. Without the idea man, there is no progress. Without the business man, there is no profit.

Idea men sometimes starve in garrets, while business men ride in fine cars. But both can be equally happy. Or equally miserable, depending on their temperament. In the long run, the idea men have the advantage. Their minds are forever in the clouds.

Applying A Tested Formula

"John, I want you to get up an ad for the Hugo French course," said Grady one day.

I went to my desk and studied past ads. Here are some of the headlines:

YOU WILL ENJOY LEARNING FRENCH
THIS FASCINATING NEW WAY

HUGO'S FAMOUS "FRENCH AT SIGHT"
24 FASCINATING LESSONS BY MAIL

LEARN FRENCH AT HOME
THIS QUICK, EASY WAY
—TRY IT 5 DAYS FREE

LEARN TO SPEAK FRENCH LIKE A FRENCHMAN
—THE FAMOUS HUGO METHOD HAS
NOW BEEN BROUGHT TO AMERICA

I thought: "If a guy can amaze his friends by playing the piano, why can't he amaze his friends by speaking French? How about a French ad based on the successful piano ad?"

I proposed this idea to Grady. I saw by the quick gleam in his eye that he liked the idea.

"Say, try that, will you!" he said.

I needed to use a situation where a knowledge of French

would be *appropriate* and where it could come as a *surprise* to listeners and where it could be displayed before an *admiring audience.*

I chose a French restaurant as the scene of action. I showed the following headline to Grady:

"They laughed when the waiter spoke to me in French."

"That's fine," said Grady, "but there is just one thing. We should not use over again the exact words 'They laughed.' Let's see if we can't find a substitute . . . They chuckled . . . They snickered . . . They giggled . . . They roared . . . They gave me the ha! ha! . . . They smiled . . . They grinned! . . . Say, how about that? . . . They grinned! That's a catchy phrase for a headline!"

Here is how the finished ad read. Note the close parallel to the piano ad:

THEY GRINNED WHEN THE WAITER
SPOKE TO ME IN FRENCH
—BUT THEIR LAUGHTER CHANGED
TO AMAZEMENT AT MY REPLY

We had dropped into Pierrot's for dinner—Pierrot's, that quaint French restaurant where the waiters speak nothing but French. Jack Lejeune, who boasted a smattering of French, volunteered to act as interpreter.

"Now tell me what you want to eat," announced Jack grandly, "and I'll 'parley' with the waiter."

With halting French phrases and much motioning of hands, Jack translated our orders to the waiter. Finally Jack turned to me.

"What's yours, Fred?" he asked.

"Virginia ham and scrambled eggs," I replied.

Jack's face fell. He knew that my order would be difficult to translate into French. He made a brave effort.

"Jambon et des—et des—" but Jack couldn't think how to say "scrambled eggs." He made motions as if he were scrambling eggs. But the waiter couldn't understand.

"I'm afraid you'll have to order something else, Fred," he said. "I can't think of the word for 'scrambled eggs.'"

I beckoned to the waiter. "I'll explain my order," I said. A chuckle ran around the table.

"Fred can't speak French, can he?" I heard a girl whisper to Jack.

"No—he never spoke a word of French in his life. But watch him. This will be funny. He'll probably give an imitation of a hen laying an egg."

A TENSE MOMENT

The waiter addressed me. "Qu'est-ce-que vous voulez Monsieur?" he asked.

There was a pause. All eyes were on me. I hesitated—prolonged the suspense as long as possible. Then in perfect French I said to the waiter: "Donnez-moi, s'il vous plaît, du jambon aux oeufs brouilles—jambon de Virginie."

The effect on my friends was tremendous. The laughter stopped. There were gasps of amazement. In order to heighten the effect, I continued for several minutes to converse in French with the waiter. I asked him what part of France he was from—how long he had been in America. When I finally let him go, my friends started firing questions:

"Fred! Where did you learn to speak French?" "Why didn't you tell us?" "Who was your teacher?"

"Well, folks," I replied, "it may sound strange but the truth is I never had a teacher. And just a few months ago I couldn't speak a word of French."

"Quit your kidding!" laughed Jack. "You didn't develop that knowledge of French in a few months."

"I have been studying only a short while," I insisted. And then I told them how I learned French without a teacher.

The above is the first half of the ad. The rest of the copy explained the Hugo "At-Sight" method and said "Try it 5 Days Free."

The coupon was addressed to Doubleday at Garden City, New York, and said:

> Please send me the Hugo 'French-at-Sight' Course, in 24 lessons, for free examination. Within 5 days I will either return the course or send you $2 at that time and $2 each month thereafter until $12 has been paid. I am to receive a copy of the French-English Dictionary without additional cost.

This ad, illustrated with a photo of a French waiter and a group of smiling people sitting at a table, was tested in full-page size in the Sunday Book Review Section of *The New York Times*.

The next day—Monday—an amazing thing happened! At least it seemed amazing to me. I was riding to the office on the subway and after glancing at the front page of the *New York World*, I turned to my favorite newspaper columnist, Heywood Broun, and started to read his column entitled, "It Seems To Me." At the top of the column was printed this line: "They grinned when the waiter spoke to me in French—but their laughter changed to amazement at my reply."

This had a dizzying effect on me. I thought, "Is this a misprint? Am I reading correctly? Am I reading this morning's *World* or yesterday's Sunday *Times*?"

Then I recalled that several times in the past, Heywood Broun had written columns in which he kidded some of the rather extravagantly worded mail order ads that were in vogue at that time.

"Naturally I was interested by this caption at the top of the advertisement," Heywood Broun wrote,

> For French has been one of the great tragedies of my life. But for French I would possess a college degree and stand among the company of educated men. Now I often cringe even in arguments where all the merits of the case are on my side. Suddenly I take thought that the man across the room, whose contention is palpably absurd, is nevertheless the holder of an A. B. from Hamilton. And so I leave the field to him with a placating "Perhaps I'm wrong," and an added obeisance of "There is much in what you say." Accordingly, I plunged headlong into the tale of the young man to whom the waiter spoke in French.

Heywood Broun reprinted the story in the ad up to the point where Fred said, "Well, folks, it may sound strange." Then Broun resumed his comments. His piece which follows, shows what an imaginative writer can do with an idea.

> Just what it was that sounded strange, I will never know, for I abandoned Fred at this point. The effect on his friends may have been tremendous, but his exploit left me cold.
> The whole anecdote left me reconciled to the fact that I am no linguist. If I had only applied myself back in college, I too might have mastered French. But to what purpose? What did his learning in an alien tongue get Fred? Ham and eggs. The end does not justify the means. The reward is not commensurate with the effort. Ham and eggs are not enough.
> But the case against acquiring French, as stated in the brief biography of Fred, is even worse than insufficient. In addi-

tion to meager returns, certain palpably evil qualities came
to Fred along with his learning. In the first place, education
made him deceitful. He was willing to sit back and let Jack
struggle and labor over the menu without ever coming to
his assistance. Calmly and fully clothed he stood on the
bank and watched his kind host flounder. Jack was his boy-
hood friend. It was Jack who saved him from the enraged
bull during that summer they spent on the farm. And it was
Jack who introduced him to Betty. Indeed, Betty and Jack
had been practically engaged until Fred came along with his
slick foreign ways.

And one of the troubles with book learning is that it often
blunts imagination and dulls a man's native initiative. So it
was with Fred. Pierrot's was a quaint restaurant and it was
up to Fred, with his equipment, to sustain the tradition of
the place. Did he call, then, for bouillabaisse and give the
name of the man who celebrated its fame, the date of his
birth and death, and his principal works? Did he demand
les escargots, and enliven the dinner table with a short
dissertation on the theory of evolution? You know he didn't.
The furthest reach of Fred's creative faculty was ham and
eggs. Bourgeois he was at heart for all his fine phrases.

All right, then, our hero is already ticketed as dull and deceitful. And in addition to that, he was a horrid, self-
centered exhibitionist. "I hesitated—prolonged the suspense
as long as possible." Those are his very words. There he sat
with three kind friends, all of whom were half-famished
after the long motor trip in the sharp November breezes.
The waiter had been informed of their simple wants and
was ready and even eager to get to the kitchen with the
orders.

One of the troubles with this quaint little restaurant—like
all quaint little restaurants—was the fact that the service was

pretty poor. Jacques Pierrot had to attend to all six tables. His wife handled the kitchen and his old grandmother acted as bartender. Henri helped upon occasion, but on this particular night he was home drunk. Did Fred show any consideration for Jacques Pierrot, anxious to be gone and about his business? Evidently not. "I continued for several minutes to converse in French with the waiter." Fred, with all his other failings, was decidedly selfish. Certainly, French conversation was no treat to Pierrot. Mme. Pierrot could talk it even faster and better than Fred.

"What part of France he was from"—that was hardly tactful of Fred. Poor Jacques blushed and stammered. He thought all that had been forgotten. After all, the verdict was "not proven" and a man is only young once.

I was stunned by this column. For a cub copy writer to have his copy get so much attention from a well-known columnist was actually frightening. I thought, "Maybe this will make them mad at me at the office because I wrote an ad that brought ridicule. Perhaps they are waiting for me right now to throw me out of the window!"

The office seemed calm on my arrival and later in the day Ev Grady said that the account executive who handled the French account was merely amused. Grady quoted him as saying, "We don't mind being kidded. We have found that the ads that are kidded are often the best pullers."

This comment ties in with an advertising axiom I heard later: "The greatest crime an advertisement can commit is to remain unnoticed." When an ad is kidded, it proves it succeeded in its primary function of *getting attention.*

It turned out that the French ad, like the piano ad, was an extremely good sales producer. And so the French ad was run in a long list of magazines and newspapers.

Humorous remarks about these two ads were made by columnists, joke writers, vaudeville artists, cartoonists and broadcasting comedians. This went on for years and has continued up to the present time. Here are samples:

HOW I BECAME A SOCIAL WOW

They grinned when the waiter spoke to me in Greek, but their laughter changed to astonishment at my reply.

"I wanna roasta bif san'wich, str-r-romberry pie, two cup skawfee!" was my simple and clear answer.

After you learn French by mail you can converse freely with anybody else who learned French by mail.

"They were surprised," remarked the gentleman who never tipped, "when the waiter spoke to me at all!"

They laughed when I stepped up to the piano. They didn't know I was from the Finance Company!

They laughed when I sat down at the piano. Somebody had taken away the stool!

They laughed when I spoke to the waiter in French—but he came right back with some Scotch.

Several magazines published complete advertisements in which the style of the piano ad or the French ad was burlesqued all the way through the copy. Here is an example:

THEY SNICKERED WHEN THE WAITER
SWORE AT ME IN YIDDISH
—BUT THEIR LAUGHTER CHANGED TO
BLUSHES AT MY REPLY

Us wandering birds had dropped into Le Mort Putois d' Amerique, that dainty little joint next to the police station where only Gregg shorthand and the touch system are spoken. Oscar McNutt, who boasted a smattering of egg on his vest, volunteered to interpret for us.

"Tell me what you want to eat," he said confidently, "and I'll 'parley' with this Frog."

With halting syllables and much arm-waving, sometimes lapsing into wig-wag, Oscar conveyed our order to the waiter. Finally he turned to me.

"What's yours, Aloysius?" he panted.

"Raw pheasant out of season, and some braised knee-joints of eels and tarnished with cheese," I gulped.

OSCAR WAS FRIGHTFULLY CHAGRINED

Oscar's false teeth rattled. That's the time I had the little fat rascal. He tried to think of the five-letter word meaning eel.

"Des epilatoires avec—avec e pluribus unum, and also die luft—et—et—" But Oscar stubbed his toe here. He just couldn't think where he'd been the night before. He tried standing on his head on the table, and started to take off his shoes and make a noise like a raw pheasant out of season. But the waiter had gone to sleep.

Everybody chortled but myself. With great savoir faire I gave smelling salts to the waiter. "I'll demonstrate," I announced. A chuckle ran around the table. Someone swatted it with a newspaper.

I held up the suspenders for several seconds—

And then I ordered Oeufs!

The waiter accosted me. "Qui etait cette fille avec qui je vous ai vu hier soir, monsieur?" he asked.

There was a pause. All eyes was on me. I waited as long as I could, then in perfect Gregg Shorthand I said: "Apportez-moi, s'il vous plait, une grande laitue pommee—et allez pondre un oeuf."

You should have seen them birds' faces!

"Where did you learn Flathead Indian?" said one of my amazed companions. "I didn't know you had a teacher."

"I didn't," was my reply, "But I met a good-looking nurse at the last boarding-house I was thrown out of."

LEARN FLATHEAD INDIAN IN FIVE NIGHTS
FREE

They sensed something new, something wonderful in me, but still they weren't convinced. "Hell! I ain't so cultured," I assured them, trying to make everyone feel at ease, and then I told them the one about the traveling salesman. They grinned when I began it, but when I finished not a head was above the table.

"You too can scratch the middle of your back without assistance from friends and fence-posts," I went on. "Just a few minutes in the clothes closet three times a week, and you can do it on your own hook."

And they all signed up for the course that same day.

You are the judge. Just fill out the coupon below for our course, "How to Play Practical Jokes on Myself," and if you don't like it, bustles are coming back.

. . . .

Laborday & Co.
Ark, Ark.

Gentlemen: Please send me on a 5-day Free Trial, at your own expense, the course entitled, "How to Operate on Yourself Without a Surgeon," for which I am enclosing check for $5.00. In case I do not like it, I will return the course and you will keep the $5.00 just as I expected.

Some Principles Learned in Mail Order Advertising

HOW TO INSPIRE COPY WRITERS

Ev Grady never criticized a single line of copy I ever wrote for him. Instead he checked with a pencil the headlines and paragraphs he liked. And praised them highly!

"That's swell, John," he would say. "Write some more like that!"

I would hurry to my desk, eager to write copy that would win additional praise. When we put together the final version of an ad, Ev simply omitted without comment any paragraphs he did not care for. Then the ad was typed in finished form by a secretary. Then the art department made a pencil layout sketch of the ad and Grady presented the copy and layout to the account executive.

Sometimes Grady had to *sell* the ad to the account executive. On some occasions I could hear Grady's voice coming over the partition of his office and telling the account executive what a good ad it was.

After that, the account executive would disappear into an inner office which I never saw. Days would pass. I was told that the account executive was presenting the ad to the client. If the client okayed the ad, I would have the satisfaction of seeing my handiwork set in nice, neat-looking type.

Those early days were fun! I worked hard for Ev Grady and enjoyed every minute of it. His method of praising good copy and avoiding criticism of bad copy was effective in getting the *best* out of his writers. He enabled his writers to retain in their copy the important quality of ENTHUSIASM.

A HAPPY COMBINATION

A big advantage I had while working for Grady was this: I was working for the man who *hired* me. There is a special advantage in this. Often you do not appreciate this advantage until you work for someone who did not hire you. Here is what I mean. The man who hires you is *on your side*. He *wants* you to make good. He is betting time and money (his time and the money he pays you) that you will make good. If you succeed, it is his success, because he selected you. If you fail, it is his failure too. And so, both boss and employee try hard to get along together. It is a happy combination.

The opposite situation often occurs in big industries and in the armed forces. People are transferred from here to there. Old department heads retire. New department heads are installed. After awhile practically nobody is working for the man who hired him. If a man fails to do well, his captain can say, "When they gave me Jones, they gave me a dumbbell. I'll get him transferred."

And Jones can say (to himself and to his associates), "The new Captain is a dope! I'm going to request a change of station!"

In a shotgun wedding of this kind, where neither party chose the other, neither one feels strongly obligated to make the marriage a success.

SOME BASIC SELLING APPEALS

"I can give you a glorious new magnetic personality so that you can influence the minds of others, attract people to you instantly, be popular and well-liked wherever you go!"

This copy from one of the mail order ads that I studied made me want to read the book on personal magnetism. In fact, one trouble I experienced in ad writing was that the ad proofs I studied were so persuasive that I wanted to read *all* the books and take *all* the courses!

One effective principle of selling that Ev Grady taught me is that people don't want to work too hard for results. "Most people are lazy," said Grady. "They want a quick, easy way to solve their problems. Listen to this paragraph:

My method releases your personal magnetism. No long course of study. No tedious mental exercises. Not the slightest inconvenience or self-denial. Just a simple, clear, age-old principle that taps the vast thought and power resources within you, releases the full sweep of your magnetic potentialities—and makes you almost a new person from what you were before.

"Sounds good," I said.

"Notice the use of the word *'releases'* " said Grady. "The method isn't work. It simply *releases* what's in you. And who is going to deny that they have resources inside of them?

"Another thing that helps to sell is the tie-in with *nature,*" Ev continued. "People believe that nature can do a lot. Take this sentence for instance . . . 'This principle never fails to work, because it conspires with *nature* to make you the dynamic, forceful, fascinating person you were intended to be.' . . . Who is going to deny that nature intended him to be forceful and fascinating?"

"Not me," I said.

THE BARGAIN APPEAL

In Chapter 2 I mentioned one of the oldest techniques of selling, namely, begin with a high price and work down to a low price. Make your proposition sound like a bargain.

Department store advertisers do this every day in newspapers and they have been doing it for fifty years. In *today's* newspapers you can find such phrases as:

Was $10 . . . *now* $5.95

Made to sell at $25 . . . *reduced to* $14.95

Mail order advertisers often use the same technique.

Now when department stores (who can measure the sales results from their ads) and mail order firms (who can measure the sales results from their ads) both agree on the same selling formula and use it again and again, it is worthwhile to remember the formula so that you can use it, if possible, in your own advertising.

Here is an incident which illustrates the effectiveness of the bargain appeal.

Not long ago I bought a piece of real estate. I got it at a price which was far less than what the real estate dealer told me was the owner's original asking price. Now the fact is that the real estate man never expected to get the original asking price. And he knew that I knew he didn't expect to get that price. This was just a little game that we played. Just a little routine bargaining which salesmen and prospects go through all the time. Eventually I bought the real estate at a price far less than the price that the realtor first mentioned.

THE VALUE OF ILLUSION

There is a good chance that I will never sell that piece of real estate. And so, for the rest of my life I can remember in the back of my head that original high price which the realtor mentioned. I can cherish the illusion that, "Well, maybe it really is worth that price or nearly that price." Then I can think of the much lower price I actually paid and feel satisfaction regarding what a bargain I got. Is there any harm in that? No. It just makes me a little happier, that's all.

In the same way, when Mrs. Brown buys a pair of gloves for 5.95 "made to sell for $10" she is just a little happier. Suppose the department store said in the ad "These gloves are $5.95 and we never expected to get more than $5.95." Would that make Mrs. Brown feel better? No sir. The department store understands Mrs. Brown's psychology. The store enables Mrs. Brown to purchase a pair of gloves for $5.95 which she can feel "were made to sell for $10." She can be just a little prouder and hold her head just a little higher when she puts on those gloves "made to sell for $10" than if she put on gloves which nobody ever claimed were worth more than $5.95. That is what you call "illusion." And life is full of illusions. It has to be. Otherwise more people would become mental cases.

Does this philosophy of illusion disturb you? Do you want everything to be according to exact specifications? If your answer is yes, I can sympathize with your viewpoint because I used to try to be factual in all things myself. I have an engineering degree from the U.S. Naval Academy at Annapolis. At the Academy we were taught to be factual right down to the last decimal point. And that teaching was correct—regarding such things as navigation, gunnery, and seamanship. In the Navy, life itself depends on accuracy in those things. But life— even life in the Navy—is not entirely made up of navigation, gunnery, and seamanship. In the Navy each man is taught to believe that his ship is the *best ship*. That belief is an illusion but it helps to keep the sailor's spirit high in war time. It helps him to polish the brass a little brighter in peace time.

AN EXAMPLE OF PRICE REDUCTION COPY

In an ad for the book on personal magnetism I found a classic example of how to create in the prospect's mind the feeling that "this is a bargain."

The copy begins by setting a high money value on instruction in personal magnetism. In subsequent paragraphs the cost is reduced a little at a time until it reaches the low, low price which the publisher is asking for the book.

I invite you to read below the paragraphs which create the bargain appeal. You may not be able to go to such extreme lengths in your own ad copy but the following excerpts will show you the method. You may remember (from Chapter 2) that the name of the author of the book is Edmund Shaftesbury.

Shaftesbury's fame was passed from one leader to another. Celebrities of the world came to him. Fees ranging as high as $500 were gladly paid for personal resident instruction at Washington, D.C.—and this for portions of his total works.

Naturally there were many people who could not attend in person, to be taught by Shaftesbury, so he was prevailed upon to put some of his methods into book form. Prices up to $100 were gladly paid for one single book.

Later in the ad, the following paragraphs occurred:

Until recently Shaftesbury's teachings have been available only to the extremely rich—people who could pay $50 or $100 each for instruction books.

But now, through the efforts of a group of his students, magnetism and its wonderful advantages are within reach of everyone. As a special introductory offer, this important work is now offered to you at the amazingly low price of only $3.

At the end of the ad was the following offer:

Read this book for 5 days. Dip into it as deep as you like. Then if you decide you cannot afford to part with it, simply remit the special price of only $3. Otherwise return the book and you will owe nothing.

The net of it is that by means of a step-by-step process, the price is reduced from $500 down to $3. And a final offer permits you to read the book for five days FREE!

The next time you write an ad in which price is a factor, why not begin by setting a much higher value on your proposition than the low, low price you eventually expect to receive?

SOME PRODUCTS DON'T MEASURE UP

"May I ask you a question?" I said to Ev Grady one day. "Sure, John."

"Well, I've been thinking that I'd like to read the book on personal magnetism."

Ev said nothing.

"When I studied copy writing at Columbia," I said, "the instructor told us to *study the product* in order to get ideas for ads. Now I've been writing about personal magnetism for some time, but I have never read the book. Where can I get a copy of the book?"

Ev didn't answer right away. He sat twisting his moustache, in deep thought.

"John, some of the boys in the copy department read the book," he said finally, "and they were not able to write such good ads about it after that. I think you had better stick to reading old ads about the book. You will find plenty of copy material in the ad files."

This incident reminds me of the story about the mail order ad for that famous book "The Autobiography of Benvenuto Cellini." The ad writer wrote a marvelous piece of copy with the headline "Swordsman, Lover, Debauchee!" A customer who sent for the book was disappointed with its contents and returned Cellini's autobiography to the publisher with this comment: "The man who wrote the ad should have written the book!"

One time an ad for a book of instruction in the rules of

etiquette appeared with the headline: "What's wrong with this picture?" The picture showed a man walking between two women on the street. The ad sold a lot of books and the head-line has been quoted so many times that it has become a famous line. But one customer wrote a letter saying that he had bought the book to find out if it was wrong for a man to walk between two women and the book did not tell him the answer. Apparently the ad writer had not read the book. He had simply used his imagination in writing the ad.

Selling without thoroughly investigating is not limited to ad writers. Some book reviews are written by reviewers who are so busy that they have only time to read the book jackets and skim through the contents. Some play reviewers leave the theater before the play is over, so that they can finish writing their reviews in time to catch the early morning editions of their newspapers. The most thrilling description of farm life I ever heard was told to me by a man who had never lived on a farm.

The skimming process is not recommended in ad writing. It is better to have plenty of time in which to do good work. And it is best to work on products which merit thorough investigation.

AN AMAZING EXPERIENCE!

The personal magnetism experience led to the following almost unbelievable incident:

The office where I worked was located near Brentano's book store. Sometimes at lunch hour I browsed around the book counters.

One day I heard a man's voice say to a book clerk: "Do you have this book?"

I looked across the aisle and saw a man holding in his hand a page torn from a magazine. Believe it or not, it was an ad I had written for the book on personal magnetism! I felt a sort of electric shock. I stood absolutely still. I watched like a bird watcher does when he sees a strange bird and does not want to frighten it away.

I remember the hopeful expression on the man's face. He was nervous, pale, unimpressive. His voice seemed weak. He looked as if he *needed* a course in personal magnetism. I recalled something Ev Grady had said: "Thousands of people are timid, colorless, self-conscious. They want to be more attractive. They envy the person who is always the life of the party."

The clerk looked at the ad and frowned. "No, we don't carry it," he said in a voice which seemed to imply disapproval of self-improvement books.

The man left the store and headed north on Fifth Avenue. I followed him. Only once in a lifetime does an ad writer see his ad actually brought into a store. I wanted to interview this chap. Questions crowded into my mind. "What caused him to look at the ad in the first place—the headline or the picture? How did he like the copy? Did he read all the copy? Why did he bring the ad to a bookstore instead of mailing the coupon?"

The chap continued walking north. I walked fast and got near him.

Then a terrible thought occurred to me. "When I tell him I wrote the ad, he will ask me questions about the book! I will not be able to answer. I will have to admit that I did not read the book. That will be embarrassing."

So I stopped following the man and watched him with a wistful eye as he disappeared into the crowd. I had lost the chance of a lifetime because I had failed to read the book!

A NEW JOB

Not long after this, I gave up my copy writing job and went to work for Batten, Barton, Durstine & Osborn, Inc. My first job had been instructive and exciting but I was anxious to work for clients whose names were better known. And I wanted to avoid those occasional situations where "if you read the book, you can't write such a good ad about it."

During my early years at BBDO, I spent most of my time on accounts that used ads with coupons to get leads for salesmen. Among these were The Phoenix Mutual Life Insurance Company, The Alexander Hamilton Institute and The Harvard Classics.

Later I worked for Liberty Mutual, Lever Brothers, Du Pont, General Electric, United States Navy Recruiting, Hormel, Wildroot, *Reader's Digest*, *The Wall Street Journal* and a number of others.

Before saying farewell to my early mail order period, I want to say that it was a great experience.

In mail order advertising you learn in two ways:

1. You learn from the men who teach you. They tell you what works and what doesn't work, based on their years of experience.

2. You learn from your own experience. Each new ad you write is an exciting adventure. You have high hopes for its success and you await the results with breathless interest. If the new ad fails, you learn something. And the lesson sticks with you. If the new ad is successful, you are very happy about it. And you try to figure out what made it successful so that you can repeat that success in future ads.

In this business of measuring results, mail order advertising has an advantage over other forms of advertising. Some forms of advertising are impossible to measure. Some forms can be only partially measured. Mail order advertising can be completely measured.

ADVERTISING THAT CANNOT BE MEASURED

For example, a man bought an expensive Steinway piano and said to the salesman: "Mentally I bought that piano ten years ago when I read a wonderful ad about it. But it was not until today that I could afford to make the actual purchase!"

How are you going to measure the delayed effect of that Steinway ad? What ad did the man actually see? What publication did it appear in? It would be impractical to keep survey men stationed in stores to overhear and record such remarks. And you could not afford to wait ten years for the results of such a survey.

ADVERTISING THAT CAN BE PARTIALLY MEASURED

Some forms of advertising can be *partially measured*. For example, you can buy readership surveys which tell what per cent of people interviewed said they saw or read your ad. You can buy listening and viewing ratings which tell what per cent of people interviewed said they heard or saw your program. But seeing and reading are not necessarily *buying*. One ad man said, "It is possible to entertain a million people without selling any of them." Therefore, even when you know what per cent rating was obtained by your ad or your program, you still don't know how many packages it sold. A low rated program could sell more goods than a high rated program

Some advertisers use sales area testing. One campaign is run in a certain area. A different campaign is run in a different area. Sales are checked by counting packages sold in stores. This method is expensive and time consuming. And it is only a partial test because other factors besides your advertising have an effect on sales.

ADVERTISING THAT CAN BE COMPLETELY MEASURED

In mail order advertising you have a *complete 100 per cent sales test*. You know exactly how much each ad cost in money. You know exactly what each ad produced in sales. Each ad is a separate, individual sales test. Each ad carries its own built-in measuring device, namely, an order blank in the form of a coupon. Therefore the mail order business has always been one of the greatest schools in which to learn how to make advertising SELL.

An Ad That Failed
— and One That Didn't

THE STORY OF TWO FAMOUS ADVERTISEMENTS
THAT WERE WRITTEN BY BRUCE BARTON

T HE TEXTBOOK for this course is 'Advertising Copy' by Hotchkiss," said Bill Orchard, copy editor of The George Batten Company, holding up the book so the class could see it.

This happened at Columbia when I was taking advertising courses to help me learn how to write ad copy.

So I bought the book. It is one of the greatest textbooks on advertising copy ever published. It has been revised and reprinted many times. Thousands of ad men and women have studied it.

On Page 6, I found the famous ad Bruce Barton wrote for the Alexander Hamilton Institute with the headline "The years that the locust hath eaten."

Reading this ad increased my desire to become an advertising writer. It helped to open my eyes to the fact that not all the world's fine writing was contained in the volume "Selections from Great Literature" which I had studied in school. Here in an advertisement, was a style so simple, so clear and yet so powerful that it rivaled anything I had read in the classics.

I invite you to read right now some paragraphs selected from this ad. After you have read these selections, I will tell you a story that teaches a lesson—a lesson that will make you a better advertising writer.

(Note: For your convenience and easy reading, the advertising selections contained in this book are printed in the same size type in which the text matter of the book itself is printed.)

In some books on advertising, the quotations from ads are reproduced in smaller type than the regular text, as if these quotations were of lesser importance. This is a disadvantage to you, the reader.

Sometimes for the sake of emphasis or clearness, it is good to print certain items in *larger* type than the regular text, or in a *different style* of type. But in no case do I want to force on you the necessity of reading smaller type than the type you are now reading.

Textbooks which are filled with quotations and footnotes in small type often suffer an ironic fate. They are read only halfway through. "You can lead a horse to water but you can't make him drink," is an old saying. It is equally true that a teacher can make a student buy a book, but he can't make him read it all the way through. That is up to the printer and the author. The printer does it by making the reading *easy*. The author does it (if he can) by making the reading *rewarding*.)

Here are selections from Bruce Barton's ad:

THE YEARS THAT THE LOCUST HATH EATEN

(Picture) Locust eating a leaf

(Note: The headline will be recognized by most readers as a quotation from the Bible. It would not be in good taste to quote the Bible in selling chewing gum or cigarettes. But in selling a two-year business course which may be a turning point in a man's career, it is quite appropriate to use a Biblical quotation. The subhead of the ad helps to further identify the quotation.)

(Subhead) In a Very Old Book Named Joel, After the Man Who Wrote It, You Will Find This Line: "The Years That the Locust Hath Eaten."

(Copy) A solemn sounding line it is, full of sad significance.

The years when there were no crops, because they were destroyed by the enemies of crops. The years when men worked and made no progress; when the end of the year found them a little poorer than its beginning, because a part of their little span of life was gone and had produced no increase.

In almost every life there are some fruitless years; but the tragedies occur, when year after year, men go along feeding their lives to the locust of indecision, or the locust of laziness, or the locust of too great concentration on a petty task.

In every week of every year the Alexander Hamilton Institute is brought into contact with such tragedies.

"I WISH I HAD ACTED EARLIER"

"My experience with the Alexander Hamilton Institute leaves me only with the regret that I did not make contact with it at an earlier time," says one man.

For that regret there is no healing. The years when one might have acted, and did not; these are the years that the locust hath eaten.

"If I had read your Course before getting mixed up in my mining proposition, it would have kept me out of trouble," another writes.

He might have read it before; the opportunity was offered to him, time after time, in advertisements such as this, but he did not act. And Fate exacted payment for those wasted opportunities, the years that the locust hath eaten.

"If I had enrolled with you a year or two ago, I should be better able to handle the problems put up to me every day," another says.

He is making progress now, rapid progress. But the progress might just as well have started two years earlier.

THE PUNISHMENT OF WASTED YEARS

This happened just the other day: A man wrote asking that someone call on him who could give him detailed information as to just how the Alexander Hamilton Institute has helped thousands of men to greater success.

The representative found a man past fifty years of age, occupying a modest position in a great corporation. He sat down to explain the Institute's plan and method. And as he talked, naming one and another who now occupy high positions, he looked across at the gray-haired man who was plainly disturbed by emotion.

The representative of the Institute turned away his eyes; he knew what that man was thinking. His thoughts were turned back over the fields of wasted opportunity; he was plagued by the thought of the years that the locust hath eaten.

The ad continues and gives background information about the Institute and ends with this urge:

To all men of earnest purpose who seek to avoid these wasted years, the Alexander Hamilton Institute comes now, asking for only one moment of firm decision—one moment in which to take the first step that can begin to turn ordinary years into great years of progress.

A book has been published for you entitled, "Forging Ahead in Business."

It is not a book for drifters; but to men who are asking

themselves: "Where am I going to be ten years from now?"
it is offered freely and gladly without the slightest obligation.

Send for your copy today.

The locust ad was written many years ago. Some years later
when I started working on the Alexander Hamilton account,
I learned to my great surprise that the ad was a failure as far
as traceable results were concerned. The Institute salesmen
loved the ad. It had class. It had prestige. The advertising department loved the ad. They were proud to publish it. It told a
great story. Teachers of advertising admired it. Ad men everywhere praised it.

But it pulled comparatively few coupons!

I could hardly believe this when I first heard it. I didn't want
to believe it! It was Ben Lichtenberg, the advertising director,
who confirmed the sad news.

I wanted to cry out: "Oh, Ben, say it isn't so! Tell me that
Daniel Webster was a poor orator!—that Charles Dickens was
a poor writer! But don't tell me that that wonderful piece of
copy—part Bible and part Bruce Barton—didn't pull!"

"The ad was a flop," said Ben.

After 31 years of copy testing, I think I know why the locust
ad didn't pull. What do *you* think? Perhaps you would like to
pause right now and think of reasons why that beautifully written message failed to bring much response? Then compare your
reasons with the following reasons. Perhaps your reasons will
agree with those listed below. Perhaps not. In copy testing, there
is always room for discussion of why a certain ad pulled or failed
to pull.

1. The headline, "The years that the locust hath eaten"
doesn't offer you anything of value. It fails to fulfill the defini-

tion of a good headline, namely, "A believable promise to the right audience." This headline fails to contain *any* promise to *any* audience.

The headline doesn't fulfil Ev Grady's rule for arousing interest, namely, "Curiosity and reward." It might be argued that the headline has a mild curiosity value but it certainly offers no reward. It might do for the headline of an editorial item because readers read the editorial items in the publications they purchase regardless of the headlines. They have confidence that the editors will give them information of value. But this confidence does not extend to the offerings of the ad writers. Readers know that the ad writer is going to give them a sales talk. Therefore the ad writers have to use headlines that have SELF-INTEREST. Or NEWS! Or strong CURIOSITY VALUE! Or SHOCK VALUE! The locust ad would have attracted more readers, and what is more important, more *prospects*, if the title of the free booklet had been used as a headline, namely, "Forging Ahead in Business."

Do you agree?

And if you agree, you must further agree that if the headline doesn't induce reading, it doesn't matter what the copy says. Because copy that isn't read, can't sell.

In the New Testament, St. Paul says in effect: "Although I speak with the tongue of an angel and I am not charitable, I am nothing." This statement can be paraphrased to fit advertising copy, as follows, "Although I write with a pen made from the quill of an angel's wing and I am not read, I am nothing."

2. The illustration which the artist gave this ad was a picture of a locust sitting on a half-eaten leaf. If ever an artist let a writer down, it was then. This picture belongs in an insecticide ad with some such headline as "Get rid of garden pests." The Institute ad would have done better with *no picture* instead of a

misleading picture. Plenty of all-type ads have done well.

Warning. Beware of art ideas that are too literal—that illustrate *words* instead of *thoughts*. Sometimes ad men forget that pictures as well as headlines should show *rewards*, or at least show *the product in action*. For example, what would some artists do in illustrating the headline "A new note in home decoration." The too-literal minded artist would show a picture of a *musical note!* The sales minded artist would have the good judgment to show a picture of a new style of home decoration.

3. The copy in the locust ad painted the dark side of the picture instead of the bright side. It stressed "what you lost" instead of "what you are going to get." Copy testing has illustrated the truth of the old saying "You can catch more flies with honey than with vinegar."

In talking to ad classes at Columbia and at New York University, and at ad clubs in various cities, I have often been asked, "Do you always have to show the bright side? Aren't there cases where scare copy, and horror copy and the dark side are more effective?"

The answer is twofold:

(a) Yes, there are cases where, for emphasis or dramatic effect, it is permissible to show the dark side. But where you have a choice between the bright side and the dark side, choose the bright side because it usually pulls better.

(b) If you do feature the dark side in an ad, be sure to quickly follow it up with the bright side.

In the latter part of Bruce Barton's locust ad there is a subhead which features the bright side of the picture in these words: "TODAY YOU MAY START FORWARD WITH THOUSANDS OF OTHERS." That is fine, but it is too late—"too little and too late." The main body of the ad is an essay on human failure. As such, it is wonderfully well done. For example, these lines:

In almost every life there are some fruitless years; but the tragedies occur, when year after year, men go along feeding their lives to the locust of indecision, or the locust of laziness, or the locust of too great concentration on a petty task.

Did anybody ever write more eloquently on the subject of wasted years? In any ad? In any book? In any poem?

But what does that copy make you want to do? I'll tell you what it makes me want to do. It makes me want to take out my handkerchief and have a good cry! I am dissolved in tears. I am so overcome with sorrow that I forget to mail the coupon!

Now, having risked my job by pointing out that an ad written by the chairman of the company that employs me did not pull, let me hasten to fill in the bright side of the picture.

In all the years that Batten, Barton, Durstine & Osborn handled the Alexander Hamilton Institute account, Bruce Barton wrote the best-pulling ads. And a lot of splendid writers worked on that account. It was a testing ground where many a copy writer's lance was broken and where many a trophy was won.

Time and again my own copy writing lance was splintered against the hard rock of readers' indifference as evidenced by insufficient coupon returns. And instead of repeating my ad, the client would dust off one of Bruce's old ads and repeat it for the ninth time and the coupons poured in.

AN AD THAT RAN FOR SEVEN YEARS

One classic ad that Bruce wrote had such pulling power that it was repeated over and over in a long list of magazines and newspapers. The ad ran for *seven years* before its coupon-getting ability was worn down to where the ad was equalled by certain other ads.

Part of this amazingly successful ad is reproduced below:

(Headline) A WONDERFUL TWO YEARS' TRIP
AT FULL PAY—BUT ONLY MEN WITH
IMAGINATION CAN TAKE IT

Why did this headline pull? You may want to think of your
own reasons first. Then read the list of reasons below:

1. The headline contains a wonderful *promise*. It offers a
great *reward*.

2. The headline is *specific*. It mentions "two years" and "full
pay."

3. The headline appeals to *men*. And men are the logical
prospects for the Institute course.

4. The headline is *cheerful*, not negative.

I think there is another powerful reason why the headline
pulled. It contains a *challenge*. The use of a challenge in advertising copy is a device which so far has not been mentioned
in this book. It is a device which Bruce Barton has used effectively many times in ads. This headline offers you something
good (a wonderful trip) and then it seems to take it away from
you (only men with imagination can take it).

This device of offering something good and then pulling it
back seems to madden men into action. It is like showing a
mouse to a cat and then drawing the mouse away. It is like
saying, "This thing is good, but are you good enough to measure
up to it?" Men who are thus challenged, apparently say to
themselves, "By golly, I'll show them I am good enough to
measure up!"

In Navy recruiting ads, before the draft in World War II,
BBDO used that appeal effectively. The headlines and pictures showed the advantages of Navy training. But the subheads
said: "CAN YOU QUALIFY?"

Below are the first paragraphs of Barton's ad. In order to

retain the proper thought sequence, I have repeated the head-line:

A WONDERFUL TWO YEARS' TRIP
AT FULL PAY—BUT ONLY MEN
WITH IMAGINATION CAN TAKE IT

About one man in ten will be appealed to by this page. The other nine will be hard workers, earnest, ambitious in their way, but to them a coupon is a coupon; a book is a book; a Course is a Course. The one man in ten has imagination.

And imagination rules the world.

I invite your attention to these points regarding the two open-ing paragraphs. The points are worth remembering because you can use them yourself.

1. The first paragraph re-states and re-emphasizes the thought in the headline. You will never lose a reader in the first para-graph by amplifying the idea which stopped him in the first place.

2. The first paragraph mentions the coupon. That is a good way to increase coupon returns. *Mention the coupon early in the ad.*

3. The second paragraph is *short*. It contains only five words. That is a good way to drive home a thought. Set the thought *by itself* in a brief paragraph. Sometimes it can be as brief as a single word! I learned the method from studying Bruce Barton's copy. From now on, it can be your method too.

Try it!

Now, how about the rest of the copy? The headline has stopped readers by making a wonderful promise. The first two paragraphs have started them to reading the message. Now what happens? Now Bruce Barton, the copy writer, faces the problem that every copy writer faces who has written a good headline. He must live up to the offer contained in the headline. He must write copy that will *justify* the headline. He must make good on his promise. And, in this case, *two* promises—

1. A wonderful two years' trip
2. At full pay

In considering this problem, please remember that the thing that is being sold is simply a correspondence course in business, consisting of a set of books and some printed lessons that are mailed to the student. How can this be described as a wonderful trip at full pay?

The answer is that the reader has to use his *imagination*. Barton gave the clue in the second half of the headline—*"only men with imagination can take it."* Here are the next five paragraphs of his copy. In reading this copy, please note that it tells *what you get* by taking the course, not *what you lost* by failing to take the course (as in the locust ad).

Let us put it this way. An automobile is at your door; you are invited to pack your bag and step in. You will travel by limited train to New York. You will go directly to the office of the president of one of the biggest banks. You will spend hours with him, and with other bank presidents.

Each one will take you personally through his institution. He will explain clearly the operations of his bank; he will answer any question that comes to your mind. In intimate personal conversation he will tell you what he has learned from his own experience. He will give you at first hand the things you need to know about the financial side of business. You will not leave these bankers until you have a thorough understanding of our great banking system.

When you have finished with them the car will be waiting. It will take you to the offices of men who direct great selling organizations. They will be waiting for you; their time will be at your disposal—all the time you want until you know all you can learn about marketing, selling, and advertising.

Again you will travel. You will visit the principal industries of the country. The men who have devoted their lives to production will be your guides through these plants in Detroit, Cleveland, Chicago and in every great industrial center.

Through other days the heads of accounting departments will guide you. On others, men who have made their mark in office management; on others, traffic experts, and authorities in commercial law and credits. Great economists and teachers and business leaders will be your companions.

There you have the description of the trip. It sounds like a wonderful trip! But before proceeding further, I invite you to note these three points:

1. Note the large number of short, punchy sentences in Barton's copy. Even the longer sentences are broken up by semicolons into short easy-to-grasp sections.

2. Note the large number of short and simple words.

3. Above all, note the frequent use of the words "you" and "yours." In the five paragraphs describing the trip, there are eighteen sentences. In *seventeen* of these sentences you will find the words "you" or "yours." The only exception is the first sentence of the first paragraph. In the last sentence of the middle paragraph, the words "you" or "yours" occur *five times*.

Since this ad was one of the best-selling ads ever written, it will be worth your while to remember these points . . . Short words. Short sentences. And YOU. *You* should use the word "*you*" in *your* copy whenever *you* write ads!

Now, let's get back to the trip. It sounds wonderful. But how about the two years at full pay? That important question has not been answered.

The answer is contained in Barton's paragraphs which follow.

The whole journey will occupy two years. It will cost you nothing in income, for your salary will go right along. Every single day you will be in contact with men whose authority is proved by incomes of $50,000, $100,000, or even more.

Do you think that any man with imagination could spend two years like that without being bigger at the end? Is it humanly possible for a mind to come in contact with the biggest minds in business without growing more self-reliant, more active, more able?

Is it worth a few pennies a day to have such an experience? Do you wonder that the men who have had it—who have made this two years' journey—are holding positions of executive responsibility in business everywhere?

This wonderful two years' trip is what the Alexander Hamilton Institute offers you. Not merely a set of books (though you do receive a business library which will be a source of guidance and inspiration throughout your business life). Not merely a set of lectures (though the lectures parallel what is offered in the leading university schools of business). Not merely business problems which you solve, and from which you gain definite practical experience and self-confidence.

All these—books, lectures, problems, reports, bulletins —come to you, but they are not the real Course. The real Course is the experience of the most successful business men in the country. For two years you live with them. In two years you gain what they have had to work out for themselves through a lifetime of practical effort.

There you have the answer! By means of imagination—Barton's imagination and the prospect's imagination—a correspondence course has been transformed into a wonderful two years' trip at full pay. Your salary goes right along because you don't have to give up your present job in order to take the course.

All I can say is—"Amazing!" If I hadn't seen it done—if I hadn't seen a mail order course transformed by imagination into a wonderful two years' trip, I wouldn't believe it was possible to do it. Every time I read the ad, I am impressed all over again. The master magician has pulled the rabbit out of the hat! And with what *enthusiasm* he writes! That is another point to remember when YOU write YOUR ads. Write with ENTHUSIASM!

Four years ago, I wrote an article for *Advertising Agency* magazine about this ad. At that time, I told Bruce, face to face, how much I admired the ad.

"I couldn't do it again," he said modestly.

He was being over-modest. He continued to do it again—in ads and in editorials. In his Sunday syndicated newspaper column with ten million circulation and in his frequent articles in *Reader's Digest,* he continued to pour out words of wisdom. He is the only writer I know of who can write mail order copy, institutional copy, and editorials with equal force.

But Bruce's remark (if it were true) illustrates an advantage which selling through advertising has over personal salesmanship. Suppose a man could write only one good piece of copy. That copy can be run in scores of magazines and in hundreds of newspapers. It can be kept going for years by the printing presses and by the broadcasting networks.

On the other hand, suppose a salesman has a good day with a prospect. That evening the salesman says to his sales manager,

"Boss, I made a sale today." The sales manager replies, "That's fine, Joe. Go out and do it again tomorrow!"

In my eagerness to comment on the "two years' trip" ad, I forgot to give you the two closing paragraphs of the ad. They are simple, dignified and effective. They start with a subhead. Here they are:

FORGING AHEAD IN BUSINESS

If you are the one man in ten to whom this page is directed, there is a book which you will be glad to own. It is called "Forging Ahead in Business." It costs you nothing, yet it is permanently valuable.

If you have read this far, and if you are at least 21 years of age, you are one of the men who ought to clip the coupon and receive it with our compliments.

(coupon)

The pictures that illustrated this ad were excellent. If ever an artist helped a writer, it was in this ad. The main picture showed a man with hat on, carrying a suitcase, starting on a trip. And just above the coupon was a picture showing a Rolls Royce automobile with a uniformed chauffeur opening the door. The caption was "The car is waiting; step in."

Marshall Ginn, who assisted Ben Lichtenberg, and who was later advertising manager of the Institute, told me that only one reader misunderstood this ad. Marshall said, "One day a man arrived at the Institute with his bag packed and wanted to know when the trip started!"

Which Appeals Succeed?
...Which Fail?

HERE ARE outline sketches of two advertisements for a course in correct English that were tested by mail order sales. One ad produced *twice as many sales* as the other ad. Can you pick the winner?

THE MAN WHO SIMPLIFIED ENGLISH (picture of Sherwin Cody) 1,000 words of copy (coupon)	DO YOU MAKE THESE MISTAKES IN ENGLISH? (picture of Sherwin Cody) 1,000 words of copy (coupon)

You may feel that in order to make an intelligent choice between the two ads, you should have before you complete copies of both ads. But this is not really the case. Because the pulling power of an ad is usually determined at a glance—at what you can grasp in the first two or three seconds during which your eyes pass across the page. Therefore, if the ad contains a good stopper (headline or picture) the chances are you have a good ad. If the stopping power of the ad is poor, you have a poor ad.

This means that in judging the comparative pulling power of two ads, your *first impression* is often more accurate than a long study in which you get lost in the details of the copy.

Judging ads is like judging people. A psychologist said, "You should remember your *first impression* of a person. It will often be a more accurate estimate of the person than a longer study will afford."

The winning ad in this case is the one with the headline: "Do You Make These Mistakes In English?"

This is one of the most famous ads ever written and has been running for more than twenty-five years. The reason the ad has been running so long is because it is a marvelous sales producer . . . because in all those years, no one has been able to write an ad for Sherwin Cody that could exceed this one in pulling power. Many experienced writers tried to write stronger pulling ads but none was able to do so. And so the old ad was run again and again. The ad is discussed here because its success teaches a lesson every advertising man or woman should know.

This ad is placed by the Schwab & Beatty Advertising Agency. My friend Vic Schwab said modestly, "Don't give us credit for writing that ad. We didn't write it. We *inherited* it from a previous agency. It was written by Maxwell Sackheim."

Not long ago, I had the pleasure of having lunch with Max Sackheim at Toots Shor's restaurant in New York and I referred to his well-known ad, "Do You Make These Mistakes in English?"

"Isn't it true that one reason the ad is successful is because the headline offers the reader a free lesson in English?" I said. "And in the first paragraph you *give* the reader a free lesson in English."

Max agreed. Then he said with a laugh, "The first time that the ad was published, it contained some mistakes in English that I didn't know about! We received plenty of letters from readers pointing out those mistakes. We corrected those unintentional errors before the ad ran a second time."

In analyzing this test, let's start with the losing headline: "The Man Who Simplified English." This headline has one virtue. It contains the phrase "Simplified English" which helps to select the right audience.

However, these words do not make it quite clear that *"here is help* in improving your English." The headline contains no "hook." It is just a plain statement of fact. It is like a title under an oil painting. The reader's reaction is "Ho! hum! . . . Is that so! . . . So what! . . . Sez you!"

The headline is written from the *wrong angle*. It is written from the angle of interest of the *advertiser*, not from the angle of interest of the reader. This is what advertising men call manufacturer's copy because it consists of a message in which the manufacturer *talks about himself*. Some writers humorously refer to this type of copy as M.B.A. These initials stand for Manufacturer's Belly Ache.

It is sometimes difficult for manufacturers to realize that manufacturer's copy is not interesting to readers. The manufacturer, who is just as human as anybody else, is interested in *himself*, in his *factory*, in his *methods*, in his *patents*, and in his *sales representatives*. Sometimes it does not occur to him that other people are not interested in these things too. He is like a golfer who gives you a long description of how he made a good shot on the fifth hole while actually you would prefer to be telling him about the good shot you made.

This seems so simple and so obvious that it should not need to be mentioned. But the fact is that it does need to be mentioned because every day a lot of manufacturer's copy is being printed and broadcast. On what kind of products? By what concerns? Not by department stores, who can check sales results from ads. You don't find many department store ads featuring pictures of the founder of the store.

In the same way, the mail order concerns who can check the sales from their catalogs, devote little or no space to telling the reader what wonderful men Mr. Sears and Mr. Roebuck were. The theme of mail order advertising and department store advertising is "Here is what we have for YOU."

Manufacturer's copy usually occurs in cases where it is difficult or impossible to check sales results from advertising. In these cases the manufacturer does not realize how much it is costing him in lost readers and lost sales when he talks about himself instead of about YOU.

At this point you may wonder why the headline "Give me 5 days and I'll give you a magnetic personality" (Chapter II) was successful. Isn't this manufacturer's copy? Yes, but with a *difference*. The manufacturer (or author, in the case of the magnetism book) is telling you what he will do for YOU.

You may wonder about the successful ad "They laughed when I sat down at the piano." Isn't this manufacturer's copy? No, this is a *story* ad. And story ads have their own special appeal. Readers buy publications to read stories. And in addition to editorial stories, they will read advertising stories if the headlines are appealing.

The headline "The man who simplified English" is not a story headline and it does not tell you what the manufacturer will do for you. It is simply a so-called "claim and boast" headline. The manufacturer is simply saying, "Look at me! Look at what I did! Look at what a great guy I am!"

Now let us examine the other headline: "Do you make these mistakes in English?" This headline illustrates important principles of successful advertising which you can use, namely,

1. It selects the right audience with the words "mistakes in English."

2. It contains the word "YOU." It is written from the "YOU" angle.

3. It offers information of value—a free lesson in English.

In regard to this last point, note the importance of the word "these" in the headline. If the headline omitted the word "these" and simply said "Do you make mistakes in English," it would suggest that the copy in the ad is simply a lecture on the value of good English. But the phrase "*these* mistakes" says in effect to the reader, "Printed below is a free lesson in English. You may get some value out of this ad without spending any money—without buying anything."

The word "*these*" does two things: (1) offers value, and (2) arouses your curiosity as to what mistakes in English are contained in the ad.

Now how are you going to apply this lesson to your own work? Are you going to apply it literally and write headlines like the following:

DO YOU MAKE THESE MISTAKES IN BRUSHING
YOUR TEETH?
DO YOU MAKE THESE MISTAKES IN PAINTING
YOUR HOUSE?

It is okay if you want to write headlines like that. They are good headlines. But I think you will advance further and make more progress if you apply a broader philosophy, if you will improvise a little, if you will apply the *spirit* of the winning headline instead of the exact wording. Write your headlines so that they will convey this thought to the reader: "*Here is some information that will be of value to you regardless of whether you buy anything or not.*" In other words, write your headline so that it offers to do the reader some good or give him some entertainment or satisfy his curiosity.

After you have stopped the reader's page-turning impulse or dial-twisting desire, you can give him the information you promised and then begin to weave in your sales talk.

Here are some successful headlines that offer the reader some value—some reward for reading the copy:

ADVICE TO WIVES WHOSE HUSBANDS
DON'T SAVE MONEY

450 NEW PRODUCT IDEAS FOR LESS THAN
2¢ EACH

HOW TO HAVE A COOL, QUIET BEDROOM
—EVEN ON HOT NIGHTS

Here are outline sketches of two advertisements for the late Dale Carnegie's famous book which has sold over four million copies.

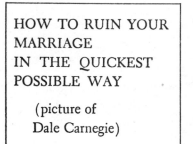

One of these ads sold twice as many books as the other. Can you guess the winner? After you have made your selection, I will tell you which ad was the winner and then list some principles which you can use in your own advertising.

Note that the above example is not quite as simple as the Sherwin Cody example. The Sherwin Cody example was simply a choice between manufacturer's copy and self-interest copy. But the above example is a choice between *two* self-interest headlines. As you advance in your study of advertising, you will find that the problems get harder. Not so often will you have to judge between an obviously good headline and an obviously poor headline. More and more often you will have to choose between two good headlines. You will have to decide which is *better?*

In this case, the winner was the ad with the headline "How to win friends and influence people." This ad, written by Vic Schwab, sold twice as many books as the other.

What can you learn from this? First let's look at the losing headline. What principles does it employ that failed to work in this case?

1. The headline attemps to be clever. It uses a reverse twist. Nobody wants to ruin his marriage. The headline forces the reader to think—to use *deduction*. It forces the reader to say to himself, "If I learn what things ruin my marriage, perhaps I can apply these things in reverse and save my marriage." Moral: Don't force the reader to think. Do his thinking for him.

2. The headline paints the dark side of the picture. The bright side is usually more attractive.

3. The headline appeals only to a married audience. This is not as wide an audience as the audience appealed to by the other headline.

4. The book offered in the coupon is not entirely a book on marriage. It is only partially on marriage. Therefore there is not a 100 per cent tie-up between headline and offer. This is important. *Make your headline select the people who are going to want the thing you are going to offer.*

Now, what are the principles employed by the headline of the *winning* ad, "How to win friends and influence people?"

1. The headline is cheerful.
2. The headline offers information of value.
3. The headline is simple, not clever.
4. The headline offers the identical article which is offered in the coupon. The title of the book offered in the coupon is "How to Win Friends and Influence People." Therefore there is no let down in interest. The headline has selected exactly the *right audience.*

Two advertisements written by Bruce Barton were tested by the Phoenix Mutual Life Insurance Company, as follows:

1. (Headline) SOME DAY YOU WILL MEET THIS MAN
   (Illustration) Picture of good-looking man.
   (Copy)

This is the story of a man who has become the servant of a great idea, who is devoting his life to making countless families more prosperous and comfortable.

(Note: The copy continued with a description of the Phoenix Mutual sales representatives. It told how they are carefully selected and trained—how you should welcome a call from one of them because of their ability to help you solve money problems through life insurance.)
   (Coupon)

"Send me by mail, without obligation, your new book, 'How to Get the Things You Want'."

Here is the other ad:

2. (Headline) GET RID OF MONEY WORRIES FOR GOOD

(Illustration) Picture of man, wife, child and home

(Copy) *Two men were talking in a club-house reading room. "Everything is going pretty well with me—now," said one of them. "I make enough money to pay the bills, enough even to take a vacation now and then. But I sometimes wonder how it would be if anything happened to me. I know perfectly well the house might be sold, my son taken out of school . . ."*

(Note: The copy continued with a description of the Phoenix Mutual plan which helps people get rid of money worries through life insurance. The copy ended with a free booklet offer in the coupon.)

One of these ads brought *three times* as many coupons and resulted in *three times* as many sales as the other ad. Can you guess the winner? The key to the answer lies in the headlines.

The winning ad is the one with the headline: "Get rid of money worries for good." This headline appeals to the reader's *self-interest*. The other headline is *manufacturer's copy*.

Here are outline sketches of two more Phoenix Mutual ads:

WHAT WOULD BECOME OF HER IF SOMETHING HAPPENED TO YOU? (picture of man looking at photo of woman) (copy) (coupon)	RETIREMENT INCOME PLAN (no illustration) (list of financial benefits which policyholders receive at age 65) (coupon)

Can you guess which of these ads produced the most coupons and sales? If so, you are a better guesser than I was.

The story of this test is amusing. I wrote the ad with the headline, "What would become of her?" And the client wrote the other ad. The client's ad was the first retirement income ad ever published by any insurance company.

At that time I felt so sure that the retirement income ad would fail to pull coupon returns that I didn't want to bother to test it. I had several reasons for my belief, as follows:

1. I didn't think that an ad without a picture would pull.

2. I didn't think that the words "Retirement Income Plan" were exciting words. Perhaps that was because I was in my twenties, and retirement seemed a long way off, especially retirement at age 65!

3. The retirement income ad contained shorter copy than the ad "What would become of her?" My mail order experience indicated that long copy usually pulls better than short copy.

4. I showed the layouts of the two ads to twenty people and asked them to indicate which ad they liked better. The ad "What would become of her?" was the winner in this opinion test.

After that, the ads were tested by running them both in the same publication and I had a staggering experience. The client's retirement income ad pulled more than *five times* as many coupons as my ad! And when salesmen followed up the coupon leads, the retirement income ad resulted in more than *five times* as many sales!

It was embarrassing to have my ad beaten so badly by the client's ad. I was supposed to be the expert! I was the advertising agency representative who worked on Madison Avenue in New York. I was supposed to be able to tell clients what was good and what was bad.

This experience taught me some lessons:

1. Clients sometimes have good ideas.

2. An idea such as "Retirement Income" can be so powerful that even with short copy and no illustration it can outpull an ad with long copy and a picture.

3. An opinion test, where you show ads to people and ask them which is best, is not always accurate. People tend to vote for ads with pictures and for ads that look like ads. At the time I made the opinion test, no retirement income advertising had appeared. Practically all life insurance advertising was based on the protection angle. The implication was that "you have to die to win." Therefore when people were asked to vote, the majority voted for *the ad which looked like the insurance ads they had been seeing.*

Another point: If a person votes for an ad that tells how he can retire on an income some day, instead of voting for an ad that tells how his wife can have money some day, there is an implication that he is a mean, selfish guy.

Experience has shown that people hesitate to vote for an ad that reflects discredit on themselves. In an opinion test of soap ads, the appeal "get rid of body odor" would never win over the "cleanliness" appeal. In an opinion test of financial ads, the appeal "how you can get a loan of $100" would never win over the "save money" appeal. Yet in a sales test, the results might be reversed.

It may seem that I am trying to discourage altogether the use of opinion tests. Such is not the case. Opinion testing can be a useful tool if used with discretion.

One advantage of an opinion test is that you can *talk to people* and ask them *why* they voted as they did. You can find out if certain headlines or pictures are confusing or misunderstood.

An opinion test is quick and cheap. It takes only a minute to ask the chap in the next office which of two pictures or head-lines he prefers. You can send out a reporter and in one after-noon get votes from twenty housewives regarding ad layouts.

But remember these warnings if you do any opinion testing.

1. An ad that sounds clever will often beat an ad that sounds simple. The reverse is usually true in a sales test.

2. An ad with a picture will almost always beat an all-type ad in an opinion test.

3. People will not vote for an ad if it makes them look bad in the eyes of the person who interviews them.

4. A radically new idea may lose out. Because people are unfamiliar with it. If you show a person two ads and say "Which ad do you like?" he may fail to vote for one of them *because it doesn't look like an ad*. But *readership tests* show that people often read a piece of copy for the very same reason, namely, *because it doesn't look like an ad*.

Here are the headlines of two more Phoenix Mutual ads:

1. MY SON IS GOING TO COLLEGE
   (subhead) By a Man Who Couldn't Go Himself

2. HOW YOU CAN RETIRE ON $250 A MONTH

The first ad told about a college education insurance plan whereby a man buys an insurance policy payable when his son reaches age 18. This plan guarantees that the son will have money to go to college some day. The other ad told about the retirement income plan. Can you guess which ad brought the most coupons and sales?

The correct answer is the retirement income ad. Reasons:

1. It appeals to a broader market. There are more people who have a retirement income problem than there are people who have the problem of financing a son's college education.

2. It is a self-interest appeal.

Here are the headlines of two ads that were tested for the Alexander Hamilton Institute:

1. HERE IS PROOF THAT INSTITUTE TRAINING PAYS FINANCIALLY

2. TO A $5000 MAN WHO WOULD LIKE TO BE MAKING $10,000

Do you want to pause and try to guess which ad brought the most coupon requests for a free booklet? And the most sales when salesmen called on the people who mailed the coupons? In these tests the number of coupons and the number of sales were almost always parallel. In a period of years I found only one case where an ad brought a lot of coupons and comparatively few sales. And in that case, the ad headline was directed to the wrong people and the copy put too much stress on the free booklet offer.

If you guessed that ad number 2 with the headline, "To a $5000 man who would like to be making $10,000" was the winner, you are correct.

Regarding this test I want to state two points emphatically:

1. Years ago when this test was run, we found that actual dollar figures in headlines are good pullers. *This is still true today.* Therefore, please remember, that if your product or service can help somebody make money, you should tell him (if you can) how much money in *actual dollars.* If your product can help people save money, then tell them a specific amount in dollars and cents. "Be specific, it's terrific!" There I go, inventing a slogan in the clever style which is usually not as effective as a simple statement such as "Be specific because it gets better results." Why is the clever style less effective? Because in the case of a clever slogan, half of the prospect's brain is devoted to thinking "How clever that is!" and the other half is devoted to thinking "How true that is!" But it is usually more

effective to have ALL of the prospect's brain devoted to thinking "How true that is!"

2. The other point I want to make is that *abstract words*
like "financially" (which is the key word in the losing headline) are not effective words. Avoid them if you can. Substitute
short, simple, basic everyday words—the words that people use
in daily conversation when they are trying to tell somebody
something and are not trying to sound fancy. Bruce Barton has
long preached the effectiveness of simple words.

The use of simple words in *broadcast* advertising is even more
important than in printed advertising. Because you are talking
to a *mass audience.* Because people cannot go back and re-read
a word they missed.

Here are the headlines of two more ads that were tested for
the Alexander Hamilton Institute:

1. ANNOUNCING A NEW COURSE FOR MEN
   WHO WANT TO BE INDEPENDENT
   IN THE NEXT FIVE YEARS

2. AN UP-TO-THE-MINUTE COURSE
   TO MEET TODAY'S PROBLEMS

Headline number 1, beginning with the word "Announcing,"
was the winner in this test by a wide margin. I think the chief
quality which this headline possesses is *news value.* It stresses
the news angle more effectively than the second headline. Also
it implies a specific benefit by using the words "be independent
in the next five years."

At the beginning of World War II, the ten largest advertising agencies were invited by the Navy to solicit the Navy recruiting advertising account. Partly because of BBDO'S
experience in appealing to men in the advertising for Alexander
Hamilton Institute and Phoenix Mutual, the Navy account was

awarded to BBDO. Here are two newspaper advertisements that were tested by means of a coupon offering a free booklet about the Navy.

1. (Headline) IMAGINE ME STEERING A DESTROYER!
   (Illustration) Picture of sailor talking to girl

2. (Headline) FREE TRAINING THAT IS WORTH $1500
   (Illustration) Picture of Navy Chief Petty Officer and list of Navy training courses.

These ads were tested in newspapers in the middle west. That territory was selected at first because Secretary of the Navy Knox told us that farmers make good sailors. The winning ad was the one with the headline "Free training that is worth $1500."

Throughout the campaign the value of Navy training was stressed and the so-called "flag waving" appeal was kept secondary. This was because the ads featuring the advantages of Navy training pulled better. This experience paralleled the previous experience of Navy recruiting officers. For years they had gotten best results with the appeal "Earn while you learn."

Here are two ads for car insurance. Both are based on the money-saving appeal but the headlines of the ads are worded differently. See if you can pick the one that brought the most coupon requests for a free booklet.

1. (Headline) CAR INSURANCE AT LOWER COST IF YOU ARE A CAREFUL DRIVER
   (Illustration) Photo of man driving car
   (Copy panel) List of specific money savings

2. (Headline) HOW YOU CAN TURN YOUR CAREFUL DRIVING INTO MONEY
   (Illustration) Photo of man driving car
   (Copy panel) List of specific money savings

The ad with headline number 1 was the winner. Why? Look at the two headlines and see if you don't agree with these reasons:

1. The first headline is simpler and easier to understand.

2. The second headline attempts to be clever. In doing this it loses clearness.

3. The first headline begins with the words "Car insurance" and therefore it immediately stops readers who are interested in car insurance.

4. The second headline omits the words "car insurance." Therefore it might be selling something other than car insurance. It might be selling a course in driving lessons. Or it might be an ad offering you a job as an automobile driver, if you are a careful driver.

Please note that if you had read the second headline *only* (without reading the other headline) the meaning of the second headline might not have been clear to you. I mention this because it illustrates a weakness that sometimes occurs in opinion tests. If you show a person a headline which makes a proposition clear and a headline which is clever but not so clear, the person will sometimes vote for the clever headline because he has the mistaken notion that advertising should be clever. Yet if you showed him *only* the clever headline he might say, "I don't understand it."

This shows how an opinion test can create a false situation whereby one headline helps to explain another. But when the ads are run in a publication, *only one headline appears at a time.*

In the same way, advertising agency men and their clients are sometimes led into the trap of cleverness that is not clear. They work on a proposition for a long time—until it is so clear and simple to them that they understand it backwards and forwards. After awhile they begin to tire of simple ways of expressing the proposition. They begin to crave something different, something subtle, something clever. They forget that the public is not so familiar with the proposition—that the public still needs to be appealed to with a simple, basic appeal such as "Car insurance at lower cost if you are a careful driver."

In this situation, a wise and conscientious advertising counselor can help his client by selling him on the idea of continuing to feature a simple, basic theme. Also in this situation a conscientious counselor sometimes *loses a client* because a new counselor comes along and offers something fancy.

Here are the headlines of two ads for General Electric bulbs. These ads were tested by running them in newspapers. Can you guess the winner?

1. WHY G. E. BULBS GIVE MORE LIGHT THIS YEAR

2. HOW TO GET MORE LIGHT AT NO EXTRA COST

I have shown these ads on lantern slides to ad classes at Columbia and at New York University. I have asked students to vote their preference regarding these ads by raising hands. Headline number 2, "How to get more light at no extra cost" usually gets the most votes. Yet when these ads were tested by including a booklet offer and by running the ads in newspapers in three cities, the other headline was the winner in all three cities.

How do you explain this? Perhaps the word "why" is a good word with which to begin a headline. But the words "how to" are also good.

Perhaps in buying electric light bulbs people consider the *cost* of the electric current to be a negligible factor.

I think that the principal qualities which the winning headline has that are not present in the losing headline are the famous initials "G. E." and the words "this year." We have found in a number of tests that names of famous companies such as G. E. and Du Pont help headlines to pull better. And we have found that putting the date or year in a headline helps pulling power. The headline "Why G. E. bulbs give more light this year" combines both of these ideas. The headline has news value. Without using the word "news" the headline conveys the idea that G. E. has invented a new kind of light bulb that gives more light. And if G. E. did it, it must be good!

You may say, "Doesn't putting the initials 'G. E.' in the headline make it manufacturer's copy?"

If so, this is manufacturer's copy *with a difference*. The manufacturer is offering you a *benefit*. He is not saying "What a great guy I am!" Instead, he is telling you that G. E. bulbs give more light this year. People have confidence in G. E. Therefore the initials "G. E." help to make the benefit *more believable*.

Five additional light bulb headlines were similarly tested but none of them contained the initials "G. E." and they were all beaten by the headline "Why G. E. bulbs give more light this year."

Having established the basic, winning appeal, we then tested *illustrations*. This was done by running in newspapers, in three cities, two ads with the *same headline* but with *different illustrations*. Here are outline sketches of the two ads:

(Picture of smiling baby)	(Picture of woman putting bulb in lamp)
(Headline) WHY G. E. BULBS GIVE MORE LIGHT THIS YEAR	(Headline) WHY G. E. BULBS GIVE MORE LIGHT THIS YEAR
(copy)	(copy)
(booklet offer)	(booklet offer)

In all three cities in which these ads were tested, the winner was the ad which contained the picture of the woman putting a bulb in a lamp.

I think this result is logical. And it is borne out by tests of illustrations on other products, as follows:

1. Pictures which show the *product in use* or pictures which show the *reward* of using the product are good.

2. Pictures which are purely attention getters and which are not related to the product are not good. A baby picture is not good in advertising electric light bulbs. It may be very good in advertising a baby food.

Here are outline sketches of two advertisements for the General Electric oil furnace:

G. E. ENGINEERS FIND A WAY TO MAKE EACH DROP OF OIL PRODUCE MANY TIMES MORE HEAT (Picture of oil furnace) (Copy) (Coupon offering booklet)

OWNERS SAVE 20% TO 50% ON FUEL WITH THE G. E. OIL FURNACE (Picture of oil furnace) (copy) (Coupon offering booklet)

These ads were identical in layout, except for the headlines. The copy in each ad was identical except for the opening paragraphs. The ads were tested in the same publication and one ad pulled *four times* as many inquiries as the other! The winner was the ad with the headline "Owners save 20% to 50% on fuel with the G. E. Oil Furnace."

Analysis:

1. The fuel bill is important as regards a *furnace*, although as we discovered above, the cost factor is not so important in the case of electric light bulbs.

2. The winning headline mentions "oil furnace" and therefore selects the right audience. The other headline does not do this.

3. The winning headline contains a self-interest appeal. The losing headline is manufacturer's copy.

4. The winning headline is simple. The losing headline is technical.

The reason that the winning headline won by such a wide margin (four times as many replies) is because it had *so many* important factors in its favor.

Here are headlines of two subscription advertisements for *The Wall Street Journal*:

1. $20 SPENT FOR *THE WALL STREET JOURNAL* MAY SAVE YOU $2,000

2. WANTED . . . MEN WHO CAN MAKE DECISIONS A MESSAGE FROM *THE WALL STREET JOURNAL*

These all-type newspaper ads were tested by including the following offer in the last paragraph of each ad:

It costs $20 a year. Or you can get a Trial Subscription . . . $6 for 3 months. Just tear out this ad and attach it to your check for $6 and mail. Or tell us to bill you. Address: The Wall Street Journal, *44 Broad Street, New York 4, N. Y.*

The winning ad was the one with the headline "$20 spent for *The Wall Street Journal* may save you $2,000." It is true that this headline contained some bad news ($20 spent) but the good news (save $2,000) was so much stronger than the bad news that the ad pulled very well. Also this headline had the advantage of selecting *prospects*. The other headline fails to do this.

Here are the headlines of two advertisements for an air conditioning unit. These ads were tested by running them in *The New York Times*. Each ad contained a telephone number and the copy invited the reader to telephone for further information. Phone calls were switched to a salesman who attempted to make a date for a demonstration, either at the showroom or at the prospect's home or office. In this way, the results of the ads were checked twice. First, by the number of phone calls and second, by the number of sales. Headlines:

1. HOW TO HAVE A COOL, QUIET BEDROOM, EVEN ON HOT NIGHTS

2. GET RID OF THAT HUMIDITY

Now it happened that the engineers who designed this air conditioning unit said that the machine's most important quality was that it reduced the humidity in a room. However, the other appeal produced more than *three times* as many phone calls and sales. I think this is because the headline "How to have a cool, quiet bedroom, even on hot nights," is simpler and more dramatic.

Please note how the use of *contrast* helps the headline. It would have been a good headline if it simply said, "How to have a cool, quiet bedroom." But the addition of the words "even on hot nights" makes the idea more dramatic and more understandable.

We also tested a headline based on the "noise reduction" appeal alone. And it did well. The idea was that if you have one of these air conditioning units in your window, you do not have to open your window to get cool air. Therefore you avoid letting in street noises. Here is the first half of the headline:

HOW TO HAVE A QUIET ROOM

Now how would you make that headline more dramatic and more understandable? What words could you add to the headline that would provide a *contrast* with the first part of the headline?

Here is how we did it: "How to have a quiet room—even if you live on a noisy street." We tested this ad and it was an excellent producer of telephone calls and sales.

I hope you will remember that formula, namely, *contrast*. When an artist wants to make a white spot stand out on the page, he puts some black around it. A preacher can make heaven sound more attractive by including a description of hell. You can make a man press forward by saying, "A reward if you do—but a kick in the pants if you don't." And in writing advertising copy, you can sometimes make it stronger by including *contrast*. I remember a successful mail order ad for a rupture remedy that used contrast. The illustration was a photo of a man doing a strenuous handspring. The headline said: "Ruptured 27 years! . . . Is this a miracle?"

Here are the headlines of two newspaper ads that were tested for a finance company:

1. WHEN SHOULD I GET A LOAN?

2. HOW YOU CAN GET A LOAN OF $100

These ads were tested by means of (1) telephone calls and (2) the number of loans completed. The ads were keyed in a simple manner which you can use if you are selling a product or service on which telephone calls are appropriate.

Here is how the method works: One of the above ads contained a panel of copy which said: "For quick information on loans, simply telephone (telephone number) and ask for Miss Miller." All telephone calls to Miss Miller were credited to that ad. The other ad contained an identical panel of copy except that the line "ask for Miss Miller" was changed to read "ask for Miss Johnson." All telephone calls to Miss Johnson were credited to the ad containing the name Miss Johnson.

In this particular test, the ad with the headline "How you can get a loan of $100" brought two and a half times as many telephone calls as the other ad.

I think the reason is obvious. In a speech at the annual convention of the American Savings and Loan Association, I summed it up this way: "The headline 'When should I get a loan?' is a philosophical headline. When a man is in trouble, he doesn't want philosophy—he wants *money!* And so he responds better to the ad, 'How you can get a loan of $100'."

In analyzing the winning headline, I invite your attention to the following qualities:

1. It is simple.
2. It is not clever.
3. It contains the word "you".
4. It is specific.

In later tests it was found that the pulling power of the headline could be increased by adding a subhead. Here is how it read:

(Headline) HOW YOU CAN GET A LOAN OF $100
(Subhead)—If You Can Pay Back $7.50 a Month

I think the moral is that people *know* they have to pay back what they borrow. Therefore they feel better when they know exactly *how much* and *how fast* they have to pay it back.

Other appeals that help to make loan ads attractive are:

1. Quick service

2. Private service

3. No inquiries of friends, relatives, or employer

Going a step further, it was found that a panel containing a list of amounts you can borrow—$100, $200, $500—plus repayment schedules for each amount—helped ads to pull better. Some banks are now featuring repayment tables in their advertising.

In this type of sales testing, you can find out other things besides which appeals are best. For example, regarding space buying, it was discovered that certain newspapers pulled more results than others. And we found that Monday is an especially good day to run a loan ad. Apparently family emergencies often occur over the week end and a loan ad on Monday attracts more prospects than a loan ad on Friday.

Here are outline sketches of two advertisements for chocolate pudding. In these advertisements there were no coupons. Instead there was a so-called "hidden offer" of a free package of pudding. This offer was not featured. It was simply mentioned in the last paragraph of each ad as follows:

"Tear out this advertisement and send it with your name and address and we will send you a sample package of Chocolate Pudding."

The reason for using a "hidden offer" instead of a coupon was to avoid requests from curiosity seekers who clip coupons to get free samples.

Here are the two ads that were tested. Both ads were run in newspapers in Hartford and Bridgeport. In each city the *same ad* brought about 60% more replies than the other ad. Can you guess the winner?

TONIGHT SERVE THIS READY-MIXED CHOCOLATE PUDDING (Picture of woman smiling and eating pudding) (150 words of copy) (Hidden offer of sample package of pudding)	HOW TO MAKE CHOCOLATE PUDDING IN 6 MINUTES (3 small pictures showing hands making pudding) (150 words of copy) (Hidden offer of sample package of pudding)

The winning ad in both cities was the one with the headline "Tonight serve this ready-mixed chocolate pudding."

Are you surprised? I was. Before this test ran, I guessed that the other ad would be the winner. My reasons were: (1) I have seen a number of successful headlines that began with the words "how to," and (2) As a rule, specific figures such as "6 minutes" help ads to pull better.

After the test was completed, the copy writer who worked on the account, gave me convincing reasons why the *other* headline, namely, the winning headline, was better.

I thought, "Well, it's easy to give reasons *after* you know the answer, but in any event I believe his reasons are correct." He said: "The winning headline gives you the pudding READY MADE. The other headline gives you the WORK of making the pudding. The illustration in the winning ad shows you the FUN of eating the pudding. The illustration in the other ad shows you the WORK of making the pudding."

I think this comment makes sense and I am grateful for it. As a matter of fact I have tried to develop a cheerful philosophy about this business of trying to guess in advance which of two ads will be the winner in a test. If I guess right, I say to myself with satisfaction, "My experience has given me *knowledge.* Hurray!" On the other hand, if I guess wrong, I say to myself, "I have just had a new experience which gave me some *NEW knowledge.* Hurray!"

If you can adopt this philosophy of "heads I win and tails I don't lose"—it will help you in many situations in business and in life. I have not yet mastered this philosophy entirely, but am working at it patiently. As one man said, "By the time I die, I will have learned how to live!"

As pointed out previously, the science of advertising is progressing. As you advance, you run into fewer situations where the choice is between an obviously good ad and an obviously bad ad. You begin to experience more situations where the choice lies between two ads, both of which contain good qualities. Copy testing is then used to determine which of two good ads is *better.*

Walter Weintz, Circulation Manager of *Reader's Digest,* expressed it this way, "Before a test is run, you have a set of logical arguments in favor of each ad tested. After the test is completed, you learn which set of arguments is stronger."

The chocolate pudding ad test is a good illustration of this. The words "how to" are excellent words with which to begin a headline. Witness the successful headline "How to win friends and influence people." Specific figures help to make a headline pull. Witness the successful headline "450 new product ideas for less than 2¢ each."

Nevertheless a headline which employed *both* of these successful formulas, namely, *"how to"* and a *specific figure,* did not do as well as "Tonight serve this ready-mixed chocolate pudding." Apparently the words "ready-mixed" contained some magic that made it the winner, even against effective opposition.

NEW knowledge! Hurray!

Here are two ads that were tested for Wildroot Hair Tonic:

1. (Headline) CAN YOUR SCALP STAND THE
   "FINGERNAIL TEST?"
   (Picture) Photo of man scratching his head
   (Copy) *There are two kinds of dandruff and Wildroot
   removes both! Etc., etc.*
   (Offer) *Send 10¢ for sample bottle of Wildroot.*

2. (Headline) GOOD NEWS FOR MEN WHO WANT
   ATTRACTIVE WELL-GROOMED HAIR
   (Picture) Man being admired by woman
   (Copy) *Now you can not only have the kind of attractive,
   well-groomed hair that means so much in social and busi-
   ness life, but you can definitely hope to keep your hair!
   Etc., etc.*
   (Offer) *Send 10¢ for sample bottle of Wildroot.*

These ads were tested in three newspapers, two in New York
and one in Chicago. In all three newspapers the ad with the
headline "Can your scalp stand the 'fingernail test'" was the
winner by a margin of about two to one.

Why did this rather shocking ad do so well? I think one
reason is because it *is* shocking. It dramatically calls attention
to an ailment which bothers a lot of men, namely dandruff,
and it offers relief. The headline seems to be negative at first
glance, but I think it has a positive implication. It implies that
if your scalp cannot pass the fingernail test, here is something
you can do about it. Also the picture of the man scratching his
head is appropriate and striking. It stops the right audience and
it stops people in a manner that is related to the product.

The "fingernail test" is not the type of copy that would win
an award for artistic excellence. It is a *selling ad*. Sometimes
advertisers have to make up their minds regarding whether they
are going to run selling ads or award-winning ads. Sometimes

manufacturers are hesitant about featuring human ailments in big print. They hesitate to call a spade a spade. But the public does not seem to be so sensitive. People who have ailments will read ailment ads and buy the products.

There is an old saying that "an ounce of prevention is worth a pound of cure." But regarding products sold in drugstores, it often seems easier to sell a pound of cure than it does to sell an ounce of prevention.

Now let's consider the appeal in the other ad, namely that well-groomed hair will help you in social life and in business life. This appeal didn't register as well as the dandruff appeal. Why is that? Don't men want to be popular socially and get ahead in business? Yes, they do. But there is the question of *believability*.

We found that the "social life" appeal worked well for Arthur Murray's dancing course. We found that the "get ahead in business" appeal worked well for the Alexander Hamilton Institute course. Perhaps it boils down to this: It is believable that a hair tonic will help to relieve your dandruff but it is not quite so believable that a hair tonic, no matter how good it is, will help you get ahead in business and in social life.

I stress this point because I think that too many advertising writers strain too hard to claim that every product or service they write about will give you sex appeal.

Psychologists have published lists of human desires and they have put the most powerful desires at the top of these lists. The lists usually read something like this: sex appeal; get ahead; health; etc., etc.

At the bottom of the list, you will usually find appeals to your public spirit, such as "how to help your town have a better park system."

Now these lists are okay, but they are sometimes misused by ad writers. The ad writer looks at the list and says to himself

"Sex appeal is tops. Therefore I'm going to use it in selling my product." And so you have campaigns which say in effect:

This soap will give you sex appeal.

This toothpaste will give you sex appeal.

This necktie will give you sex appeal.

This shoe polish will give you sex appeal.

These eye glasses will give you sex appeal.

Moral: It is okay to look at a list of appeals in order to find a good one for your product. But use judgment. Select the best appeal that is also logical and believable. Select an appeal that will really make sales. Don't try to sell everybody and end up selling nobody. In shooting big game it is better to use a rifle bullet that will knock one animal dead than to use buckshot that will merely pepper the whole flock.

Here are headlines of two ads that were tested for Wildroot Hair Set for women:

1. GIRLS! . . . WANT QUICK CURLS?

2. DOES HE STILL SAY, "YOU'RE LOVELY?"

The experience gained on the previous test of Wildroot ads that appealed to *men* is paralleled by this test on a different product. The ad with the headline "Girls! . . . Want quick curls?" pulled three times as many requests for samples as the other headline.

Here is an analysis of the winning headline:

1. The word "Girls" helps to select the right audience.

2. The offer of "quick curls" is simple and believable.

Here is an analysis of the losing headline:

1. It is not as specific as the winning headline.

2. It appeals to an older audience.

3. It is not as believable to say that this product will make

men say "You're lovely" as it is to say that it will give you quick curls.

Incidentally, in writing headlines, don't underestimate the value of beginning a headline by naming the people you want to reach. I recall the many ads that have been run by magazine publishers attempting to get boys to sell subscriptions by offering the boys prizes and rewards. The headlines read like this:

BOYS! . . . GET THESE ROLLER SKATES

BOYS! . . . THIS AIR RIFLE IS YOURS

I used to think, "Can't the ad writers invent something more original than to begin every headline with the word 'Boys'." Then one day the advertising manager of a magazine showed me the results of testing a number of different ads appealing to boys. After that, my reaction was, "Yes, the ad writers can think of plenty of devices besides beginning every headline with the word 'Boys', but nothing gets such good results as the simple, long-used word 'Boys'."

Here are two all-type ads for a hand lotion that were tested in newspapers with a hidden offer of a free sample of the product:

1. (Headline) HUNDREDS ARE CHANGING TO THIS HAND LOTION
   (Copy) *Are your hands rough, red, cracked. There is quick relief, etc., etc. . . .*

2. (Headline) POPULAR SECRETARY CAUGHT RED HANDED
   (Copy) *Too bad she didn't know there's quick relief for rough, red, cracked hands, etc., etc. . . .*

I just want to state two points regarding this test.

1. A number of times I have shown these two ads to ad classes at Columbia and at New York University and each time the ad "Popular Secretary Caught Red Handed" gets an appreciative laugh at its humor and it gets the most votes from students.

2. The other ad was the winner on sample requests.

This situation explains why so-called clever ads are sometimes published for products where it is impossible to check sales results from ads. The copy writer is a human being. He likes to produce ads that will get praise from his friends and associates. The account executive is a human being. He likes to give his client an ad which the client will get a kick out of. The client is a human being. He likes to run ads that his friends and associates will say are clever. And so the clever ads run and everybody is happy.

But what happens when an ad with a headline such as "Popular Secretary Caught Red Handed" appears in a publication. Two things happen, as follows:

1. There is a group of women who want a hand lotion that will relieve red hands, but few of them read any further than the headline "Popular Secretary Caught Red Handed." Why don't they read the copy? *Because they don't know that this is an ad for a hand lotion.*

2. There is a group of women whose curiosity is aroused by the headline. They think they are going to read some sort of detective story. But they soon discover it is not a detective story. It is an ad for a hand lotion. And so most of these women quit reading. But a few continue to read and a few are sold. These are the women who wanted a detective story but who also want a hand lotion.

Now what happens when the *other ad* appears in a publication and women read the headline, "Hundreds are Changing to this Hand Lotion"?

Two things happen:

1. Women who don't want a hand lotion don't read any further. So what! Who cares! Your copy might not have sold many of them anyway because these women have a high sales resistance regarding a hand lotion.

2. Women who want a hand lotion read the copy. And they get just what they want and expect—information about a hand lotion. And a lot of them are sold. Because the headline *selected good prospects and eliminated bad prospects.*

Why do advertisers sometimes run so-called clever ads that fail to stop prospects and that disappoint most of the readers who do read the copy? Well, as mentioned above, the clever ads are run mostly for products where the sales results from the ads cannot be checked. Furthermore the clever ads do make *some* sales. And they satisfy the urge of ad men to run clever ads that get praise from friends and associates. I am not defending this situation. I am simply trying to explain how it comes about.

When the now famous canned meat called Spam was first introduced, a number of different advertising appeals were tested. They were tested by stating each appeal in the headline of an all-type advertisement. The story of this test was told in a brochure prepared by Henry Haupt, head of BBDO's Chicago office. Here are three of the headlines that were tested:

1. WHAT'S NEW IN SUMMER SANDWICHES?

2. HEARD ABOUT THOSE NEW CANAPES?

3. GUESTS FOR SUPPER? WHAT SHALL I GIVE THEM?

Here is the copy. The same copy was used for each of the three headlines:

A *marvelous new kind of meat! Comes in a can . . . ready to
eat . . . keeps fresh on a pantry shelf. Slice it cold . . . or heat
it. '101 uses'. Convenient, tasty, economical, quick. For full size
35¢ can and recipe booklet, tear out this ad and send it with
10¢ to cover mailing, to Food Dept., 1421 N.W. Bank Building, Minneapolis, Minnesota.*

Now glance back at the three ad headlines and see if you
can rank them in the order of their pulling power. If you ranked
them in the following order, you are correct:

1. WHAT'S NEW IN SUMMER SANDWICHES?

2. GUESTS FOR SUPPER? WHAT SHALL I GIVE
THEM?

3. HEARD ABOUT THOSE NEW CANAPES?

Analysis:

1. The winning headline contains the word "new." It is
timely because it mentions the word "summer," and these ads
were tested in the summer. A sandwich is a well-known item of
frequent use. And Spam is logical for making sandwiches.

2. Regarding the headline, "Guests for Supper," perhaps
Spam is not such a logical item for serving guests. Or perhaps
the average housewife does not as often have occasion to serve
guests as she does to make sandwiches.

3. Regarding the headline about "new canapes": This headline
contains the word "new" which we know is a good word. Yet
the headline ranked last. How do you explain it? I would explain it by saying that canapes are an item of infrequent use
with the average housewife. Therefore news about canapes is
not as important as news about sandwiches. In judging appeals
like this you cannot always be guided by your own experience.

Maybe you serve canapes and cocktails every afternoon in your home. But the average housewife does not.

Here are two headlines that were tested for canned beef stew. The ads were all-type and each ad contained a hidden offer of a sample can of beef stew.

1. TASTES BETTER . . . COSTS LESS

2. ONLY 25¢ A SERVING

The winning appeal, by more than two to one, was "Only 25¢ a serving."

I mention this in order to illustrate again the pulling power of a *specific figure*. The losing headline contains *two* appeals, (1) Taste, and (2) Price. But these appeals are stated in *general terms*, not specific terms. The winning headline contains only *one* appeal, namely, price. But this appeal is made *specific* by using the words "25¢ a serving."

Here are two headlines that were tested by a manufacturer of wall board for people who want to improve their homes. Each ad carried a coupon offering a booklet containing "Do-it-yourself" information.

1. BUILD AN EXTRA ATTIC ROOM

2. BUILD YOUR OWN DARKROOM

The winner was headline number 1, "Build an extra attic room."

This result simply illustrates that there are more people who want extra attic rooms than there are amateur photographers who want darkrooms. Both of these headlines are so-called "rifle bullet" headlines, aimed at specific groups. But one headline is aimed at a bigger specific group than the other.

WHICH APPEALS SUCCEED . . . WHICH FAIL

We have studied a number of tests. We have tried to guess the winners before we knew the actual results. Part of the time we guessed right. Part of the time we guessed wrong. But right or wrong, we always tried to learn all we could from each test. Like squeezing an orange, we tried to squeeze every drop of value out of every test. Why? Because these tests cost money. Because these tests take time. Because we want to learn principles about human nature so that we can produce advertising that sells. So that we can start future tests from a higher plane. So that we can avoid re-testing obviously poor appeals. So that we can select good appeals in those cases in the future where we do not have time to do any testing.

Here is a list of tested appeals. It is based on 31 years of copy testing experience. Actually it is based on more years than that, because some of this knowledge was inherited from previous generations of advertising men.

1. Appeal to *self-interest.* The person who reads your ad or who hears your broadcast is thinking along these lines: "What have you got that will do me some good?" You will recall that the self-interest appeal was the most frequent device employed by almost all of the winning headlines. For example, "How to win friends and influence people" . . . "How you can get a loan of $100" . . . "How you can retire on $250 a month."

2. Select the *right audience.* Remember, for example, that the winning ad on car insurance was the one that had the words "car insurance" in the headline.

3. Make your advertising *easy to understand.* That can be a life work in itself—learning how to write simply. Many people go through their entire lives without making themselves understood. Some of the world's greatest books remain unread on the

shelves because they are hard to read—books with great philosophies that would help you and me in our daily lives. But we don't bother to read these books because the ideas in them have to be dug out with a mental "pick and shovel."

4. *Give news.* If you have news, tell it. Tell it fast. Tell it with force. Tell it often. And keep on telling it. The news about your new product will be news to the public, long after it is old stuff to you and to your salesmen and to your dealers. Announcement ads about the new Alexander Hamilton course were the best pullers for two years. Announcement ads about new instant Maxwell House Coffee ran for five years, with excellent sales results. Spreading the word about new products and services and about improvements and new uses of old products will always be one of the strongest selling types of advertising.

5. Make your advertising *believable.* For example, the phrase "if you are a careful driver" helps to make more believable the offer of "car insurance at lower cost" because it gives a valid *reason why* car insurance can be sold at lower cost to certain people. Other aids to believability are testimonials and money back guarantees. Believability is so important that it will be discussed at greater length in a future chapter.

6. Offer *quick results.* For example, a successful headline said, "Tonight serve this *ready-mixed* chocolate pudding."

7. *Be specific.* Retirement income advertisements which named specific sums of money pulled better than retirement income ads written in general terms.

8. *Arouse curiosity,* if you can do so without sacrificing clearness. For example, curiosity is aroused by the headline: "Do you make these mistakes in English?"

9. *Give the reader or listener something of value,* in exchange

for his time. In that way you will *hold his attention.* For example, the above mentioned ad, "Do you make these mistakes
in English?" gives the reader something of value in exchange for
his time, namely, a free lesson in English.

10. If you are writing advertising for a famous manufacturer,
it will help the pulling power of your copy to feature the manufacturer's name *plus a reward.* For example, "Why G. E. Bulbs
give more light this year." And if your client is not famous, you
may want to feature his name anyway in order to *help make
him famous.*

I want to say one last word about the self-interest appeal—
which is the most important appeal of all. I recall one time
when I lectured to an advertising class on the subject of advertising and my father was sitting in the audience. I stressed the
importance of the self-interest appeal and after the lecture
my father said, "You make the world sound rather heartless
with so much stress on self-interest."

I could understand his point of view. I felt a little bad about
showing in his presence the exhibits where the self-interest
appeal outpulled the altruistic appeal. I felt the same way the
time a minister sat in the classroom and heard a lecture I gave
at New York University. I hated to do anything that might
disturb his belief in a beautiful world where everybody loves
everybody.

My father was an idealist. He studied medicine, got a degree
and spent his life curing people's ailments. He always believed
in doing the *right thing* rather than the self-interest thing. He
used to treat a lot of charity patients as well as paying patients.
I recall how it used to annoy my mother (a practical person)
when father would treat a charity patient before a paying
patient, just because the charity patient arrived in the waiting
room first. But father held to the rule of first come first served,

regardless of whether they could pay. And at election time he used to study the editorials of both Republican and Democratic newspapers so that he could vote for the *right candidate*, not just the candidate that appealed to him personally.

I mention the above merely to illustrate the fact that I understand and admire the altruistic point of view even though I cannot advocate it in selecting advertising appeals.

You have to face facts if you are going to stay in business. There are simply not enough altruistic people in the world to make altruistic ads pull as well as self-interest ads.

Even religious leaders recognize the power of the self-interest appeal. Religious leaders try to teach people to behave properly. They say, "Be good." But this is not sufficient. And so they say, "Be good and *you will get your reward.*"

In politics it is the same way. A politician friend of mine summed it up by saying, "People vote where their interests lie."

And so, while we are all working and striving and hoping for a better world, we must, for the time being, recognize the world as it actually is. We must realize that people are looking for ways to help themselves and better themselves and we will get the best results if we appeal to them along those lines.

9

How to Think Up Ideas

THERE ARE various techniques that can help you to think up ideas. These techniques can be applied to many things such as thinking up new inventions, plots for stories, titles for songs, etc. In this chapter I would like to discuss the application of idea-producing techniques to the writing of ad headlines.

"Mail order experience shows that the most important part of an advertisement is the headline," said copy chief Ev Grady.

During my apprenticeship as a copy writer, Grady used to hand me ad layouts with the headline lettered in with a pencil across the top.

"Here is a layout, John," he would say. "Please write copy for this ad."

Thus I was *doubly impressed* with the importance of head-lines. First because the boss said that headlines are important. And second, because in the beginning *I was not allowed to write headlines.* That is one way to make an impression on a young man. Just say to him in effect, "Here is a task you are not equal to."

And so, as an ad writer, I spent a lot of time working on *headlines.* I wrote long lists of headlines. Sometimes I wrote *pages* of headlines. I didn't want to be a writer of small print only. I didn't want to merely fill in space beneath somebody else's headline. I wanted to write headlines too.

Experience over the years shows that Ev Grady was right

about the importance of headlines. For example, not long ago we made a copy test on a drugstore product, as follows:

1. We tested, with a hidden offer, a series of ads with the same copy but different headlines. The extreme difference between the pulling power of the best headline and the poorest headline was more than 400 per cent.

2. Then we tested some ads with the same headline but with different copy in each ad. The difference between the best pulling copy and the poorest pulling copy was 50 per cent. In other words, the headline made eight times as much difference as the copy.

I think the moral of this is that if you don't have a good headline, you have "missed the bus." You are as helpless as a salesman whose prospect has boarded a vehicle and driven off and left the salesman standing on the curb.

The above refers to advertisements that are printed in newspapers and in magazines. But how about television commercials and radio commercials? How about direct mail advertising? Do these forms of advertising have headlines? The answer is yes. Perhaps instead of the word "headline" you may prefer the word "stopper." All forms of advertising have "stoppers."

In a TV commercial or a radio commercial, the headline or stopper is the opening remark of the announcer. This remark decides whether you will listen or let your mind drift to other things—whether you will stay by the broadcasting set or take the opportunity to go to the kitchen for some more ice.

In a direct mail advertisement which is delivered to you by the postman, the first message you see is the headline or stopper. This may be the first sentence of the letter. Or the headline on a circular. Or a sentence printed on the envelope. It is this first impression that decides whether you will read the letter or throw it away.

Therefore, ad writers had better learn to think up good headlines, good stoppers, arresting devices, and interrupting ideas that grab hold of people's attention and make them read or listen.

USING PICTURES AS STOPPERS

Sometimes it is not words but a picture that decides whether or not people will pay attention to your message. But the idea for the picture is usually furnished by the writer. Or the picture is simply an illustration of the headline which the writer wrote. For example, the headline "They laughed when I sat down at the piano" was illustrated with a picture of some people laughing as a man sat down at a piano.

An exception to the above situation was described by a friend of mine who worked for an advertising agency where *an artist was president of the agency.* In this organization almost all new ads were originated in the *art department* instead of in the copy department.

"The artists made up the ads" my friend said. "They made layouts which called for *big pictures* and *small copy*. A small empty space was left in the layout for the copy. Copy writers were instructed as follows: 'Don't write too much copy. Write just enough to fill this space.' Sometimes headlines were not permitted. The copy department was humorously referred to as the 'gray wash' department because the copy writer's contribution to an ad was simply a small rectangle of type, which to an artist's eye, looked like a block of 'gray wash.' "

The above is *not typical*. In most agencies, the ads are originated in the copy department. The writers produce the headlines and the copy and then take the ad to the art department to get a layout. The artist reads the ad, thinks up an illustration idea (or uses the writer's illustration idea) and makes a layout.

The same system is usually used in producing radio commercials and TV commercials. In radio, the writer writes the commercial. Then music or sound effects are added. In TV, the writer writes the commercial. Then the visual action is added.

In discussing the question of how to get attention—how to stop people with an interrupting idea—we will discuss printed advertising mostly. For three reasons:

1. More scientific facts are known about printed advertising than about broadcast advertising. Experiments have been going on for a longer time.

2. Printed copy tests are subject to more accurate controls.

3. What you learn about human nature in experiments with printed advertising can be pretty generally applied to broadcast advertising. For example, if the phrase "only 25¢ a serving" is more effective than the phrase "costs less" in a printed ad, it will also be more effective in a broadcast commercial.

AIDS TO YOUR CREATIVE THINKING

Let us say that you are about to sit down to write an advertisement. A good way to start is to begin by writing headlines or stoppers.

One reason is because it is *easy* to start that way. You can start while your mind is cold. You simply dash down on a piece of paper the first words about the product that come into your head.

If you are writing an ad for a corn remedy, you can start by writing down the word "corns." Then you can write down the next words that come into your head. Perhaps the words "corn gone." Or maybe you will jot down an idea for a *picture*.

Then write down the next words that come into your head. And so on. Each phrase or sentence you write down is a possible headline or picture idea. Not all of these ideas will be good. Not all of them will be bad. Later you will decide which ideas to use. Or you can make an opinion test. Or an inquiry test.

As you write, your mind warms up. You write faster and easier after awhile. It is like shovelling snow. Chilly work at first. Your muscles are awkward. Your hands are clumsy. But as you keep swinging that shovel, it gets faster and easier.

Time passes . . . Pretty soon you begin to tire. New ideas come into your head less often. Finally you have no new ideas at all. You have written down everything you can think of.

BOOSTER TECHNIQUES

Now is the time to use *booster techniques*. You can take a walk to the water cooler and let your mind rest for a minute. Perhaps a cup of coffee would be good. One way to get your mental motor going again is to go through the client's scrapbook of old ads. On most products, unless they are brand new, you will have previous advertising material which you can review. Study any available records of results such as coupon returns or inquiry records or readership reports.

Pay special attention to ads that did well. You may find a key that can be adapted to fit present conditions. I recall how Leslie Davis and George Delaney of *The Wall Street Journal* were favorably impressed when we studied the mail order subscription sales records of their old ads and made charts of the results. Years later Les said: "We felt that our advertising was in good hands because before you spent any money, you tried to get additional value out of money already spent."

COLLECTING COPY MATERIAL

In writing down all the ideas you can think of, you are really doing *two jobs*. In addition to collecting headlines and picture ideas, you are also collecting *copy material*. Because you will eventually write down more headline ideas than you can use in an entire campaign. Some of your headlines can be used as sub-heads. Some of your illustrations can be used as sub-illustrations. Some of your headlines can be used as opening sentences of paragraphs. Or developed into whole paragraphs. That is one of the advantages of starting by writing headlines. It is easy to jot down phrases that pop into your head or that pop out at you from previous ads.

As you continue to write, you will find that you are developing some of your phrases into sentences and some of your sentences into paragraphs. That cold motor (your mind) which was stalling and backfiring at first is at last warmed up to the point where it can climb hills.

SOURCES OF IDEAS

Study the client's direct mail advertising in addition to his space advertising. Read his booklets, leaflets, circulars, sales letters, broadsides, and brochures. Here you will find long copy and therefore lots of ideas to choose from. Perhaps in small print in some old booklet you will find an idea that can be modernized and used right now.

Study the product itself and the package and everything printed on the package and any literature enclosed inside the package. Perhaps you will find a hook on which to hang a campaign. Some products are so similar to competitive products that you have to sell the beauty or the convenience of the package.

Talk with the sales people who are selling the product or service. Talk with people who use the product. Take notes on what they say. If note taking causes them to talk less freely, you can wait until you are alone and then write down everything you can remember. The basic theme of an effective insurance campaign came from a salesman who had found that this theme was a good sales getter.

Talk to the technicians who make the product. Gerard Lambert and Milton Feasley who started the well-known Listerine campaign first heard the word "halitosis" from a chemist employed by the Lambert Pharmacal Company.

Read scientific literature about the product. Claude Hopkins, in his book "My Life in Advertising," told how he searched for an appeal for Pepsodent Tooth Paste: "I read book after book by dental authorities on the theory on which Pepsodent was based. It was dry reading. But in the middle of one book I found a reference to the mucin plaques on teeth, which I afterwards called the film. That gave me an appealing idea." The Pepsodent campaign "remove that dingy film" became famous.

Perhaps you can re-work an old but successful formula. Long ago Bruce Barton invented for Vogue magazine this headline: "$2 spent for Vogue may save you $200." This headline was so effective that it continued to be used for years. Barton said: "The argument was that the really expensive gown or hat is the one a woman buys but never wears, because she discovers, after paying for it, that it is not in style. Every woman has had such an experience; the appeal was universal." Not long ago we found that an adaptation of this appeal worked successfully for a different publication (as mentioned in Chapter 8), namely, "$20 spent for The Wall Street Journal may save you $2,000."

ANOTHER SOURCE OF IDEAS

When you have exhausted the possibilities of studying the client's printed literature and talking with salesmen and technicians, you can sit down with a pile of newspapers and magazines and turn pages and make notes regarding ANY pertinent ideas that are suggested to you by what you see and read.

For example, you may see a telephone number in a department store ad and alongside the number you may see a small picture of a telephone. You say to yourself, "That's good. We are printing telephone numbers in our newspaper ads. We can increase the urge to telephone by including a picture of a telephone in our ads."

You may say to yourself, "We will do even better than that. We will show a picture of a telephone and a smiling, friendly-looking operator answering the telephone."

You may say, "We are not using telephone numbers in our ads but we are including a printed order form which we want people to fill out. So instead of a picture of a telephone, we will show a picture of a hand holding a pencil and filling out the order form."

Thus there are three ways you can use ideas you see in other ads, as follows:

1. Copy the idea as it is.

2. Improve the idea.

3. Adapt the idea in a new and different form.

You may say at this point: "But I don't want to copy anybody else's ideas. I want to invent my own ideas. I want to be an original thinker. Original thinkers never copy."

There are three answers to that:

1. Go ahead and originate all you want. That is part of your job. However, unless you also grab good ideas, from whatever source, you will be handicapped in your battle with competitors. Because competitors will grab your good ideas as fast as they appear.

2. Your client is not paying you to be solely an original thinker. He is paying you to make money for him—to help keep his factory going.

3. It is not true that original thinkers never copy good ideas. Shakespeare copied from old ballads the ideas for many of his plays. Benjamin Franklin not only copied many ideas but boasted about it in his autobiography.

In searching for ideas, in your own head or in other people's heads, remember to keep pencil and paper handy. Write down ALL ideas. Good ideas. Bad ideas. Half-formed ideas. Outlandish ideas. Select the best ideas later. Alex Osborn pointed out in his book, *Your Creative Power*, that if you stop (while you are in the creative stage) to consider whether an idea is good or bad, you may end up just where you started, namely, with a blank sheet of paper.

Important: Put into a file marked "Copy Data" all your lists of headlines and all your notes on ideas for copy and illustrations; also any clippings or helpful literature you may have collected. From time to time in the future, you will put into this data file any scribbled notes of ideas, any new headline thoughts, any pertinent items torn from your daily newspaper. Then when you have to write an ad, and your mind is blank, you will take out your copy data file and it will be immensely valuable.

IDEAS THAT COME AT ODD MOMENTS

After you have worked on a copy writing problem for a while, you will find that nature comes to your aid and adds a new locomotive to your train of thought—namely, *your subconscious mind*. Headlines and copy ideas will pop into your head at odd times—while you are going to sleep at night, while shaving, while riding to work, while reading, while taking a walk. You will imagine that your mind is thousands of miles away from the copy problem you were working on yesterday. Then suddenly, there it will be—an idea you may be able to use. Sometimes it will almost seem to be printed in bright letters across the inside of your head. Sometimes you will think of several ideas in rapid succession. Now is the time to act fast. You must have paper and pencil *with you*. You must start writing immediately. And I mean *immediately*. Don't delay. Don't put it off. Get that pencil going within ten seconds. The ideas that flowed into your brain so easily and pleasantly and without warning will flow right out again, like water through a sieve.

On those rare and delightful occasions when you are blessed with *several ideas in rapid succession* you may sometimes lose one of them because you cannot act fast enough. While you are writing down the first idea, you will feel the other ideas slipping, slipping, slipping. One thing that helps is this: Don't attempt, in making notes, to write whole sentences. Think of a single word that will remind you of the idea and jot it down. Then go on to the second idea and nail it down with a single word. And so on. Later you can go back and elaborate.

THE STORY OF A PHOENIX MUTUAL ADVERTISEMENT

I recall thinking of a Phoenix Mutual headline one night while walking along Broadway near 110th Street. For weeks I had been turning over in my head the successful all-type Phoenix Mutual ad with the headline "Retirement Income Plan" (referred to in Chapter 8). That ad was getting excellent results, but eventually its coupon pulling power would be worn down by repeating the ad over and over. What new ad could we run in its place that would be just as good, or better if possible? I needed a headline. And I wanted an illustration idea. The all-type ad was fine, but who knows maybe there was some kind of picture that would make the ad even better.

One evening about 9 P.M., while out for a walk, I thought of the words "quit work." These words conveyed the same idea as the word "Retirement." Perhaps the words "quit work" were even better because they were simpler and easier to understand. I stopped by a lighted store window and wrote on a piece of paper the words "quit work" and walked on.

I realized that I did not have a complete headline but merely some key words around which a headline might be built. As I walked on, I thought of one of Bruce Barton's formulas for starting a headline, namely, begin with the words "To the man" or "To the woman." This formula had worked successfully for several advertisers. For example, Bruce Barton had written a strong-pulling ad for the Alexander Hamilton Institute with the headline, "To the man who is 35 and dissatisfied." So I wrote down the headline "To men who want to quit work."

But there was something wrong with my headline. It suggested quitting work right away, not at age 65. But I didn't want to put age 65 into my headline. Age 65 seemed too remote. Besides, a headline containing this phrase had already been tested and it brought mediocre results. The headline was "When you are 65 we put you on our payroll."

A few blocks further on I thought of the words "some day" and wrote them down, making the headline read "To men who want to quit work some day." This seemed like a complete headline, and possibly a good one.

How about a picture? How do you show a man not working? Do you just show him standing with his hands in his pockets? Not very exciting. Then I thought of the idea of a picture of a man fishing. So I wrote down the word "fisherman." If a chap is fishing, he can't be working. Therefore the picture says "quit work." And fishing is fun. And it has a broad appeal. Plenty of fellows like to go fishing.

The next day I wrote the copy. It started off as follows:
This page is addressed to those thousands of earnest, hard-working men who want to take things easier some day. It tells how these men, by following a simple, definite plan, can provide

for themselves in later years a guaranteed income they cannot outlive.

A layout was made for this ad. The copy and layout were approved by the client. We decided to insert in the center of the ad a panel of copy with the heading "Retirement Income Plan." In this way we would add to the new ad some of the power of the successful old ad. If the new headline was good, its effect would be increased by the words "Retirement Income Plan" printed on the page. If the new headline was poor, the new ad would be saved from utter failure because it contained a brief panel version of the successful old ad. *Please remember that technique.* Let your new ad be helped by including, in a panel, a cut-down version of a tested ad. We used that technique a number of times with good results.

HELP FROM A PHOTOGRAPHER

I recall having lunch with the photographer we hired to take the fisherman picture for the ad, "To men who want to quit work some day."

"You could take the picture on one of those empty docks along the Hudson River," I said, remembering the many fishermen I had seen there while I was canoeing on the Hudson.

"Oh no, not that!" exclaimed the photographer in dismay. "That would make a bum out of the fellow! I've got to take him out in Jersey somewhere and find a nice lake with some nice trees and grass. I've got to borrow some of that fancy fishing tackle from Abercrombie's—you know, rod, reel, basket. This chap has to look well-to-do. Not one of those hoboes that sit all day with a worm on the end of a string. I've got just the right model for you. And he doesn't charge much. A retired policeman. You know, policemen often have good faces. Good, strong, regular features. They don't worry much. So they have pleasant expressions. You'll like this fellow."

"Have another drink," I said. "And do it your way. I think you're right."

Well, the picture was taken and it was a dandy—except for one thing—the cop was not smiling. He had a fine face but in all the picture shots he looked serious. And in most of the shots he was looking at the lake instead of into the camera.

"We want him to smile and look directly at the reader," I said.

"Holy mackerel," said the photographer. "We tramped all over Jersey looking for that location. We can't do it again. We spent a whole day! I don't know if we could even find the same spot. I'll tell you what I'll do. I'll get him to smile while he is sitting on his back porch at home. I'll shoot just his face. Then we can cut his face out and paste it over the other face. I guarantee you it will look okay."

It did look okay. In fact, it looked swell! The policeman, with his big genial smile and the blissful lakeside surroundings seemed to say that retirement is wonderful, that Phoenix Mutual is wonderful and that all is right with the world!

This ad was tested and did extremely well. On coupon returns and sales it beat the client's winning all-type Retirement Income ad by a good margin. You will recall my embarrassment (Chapter 8) when the client's ad beat my ad so badly. It is all right to have the client's ad beat yours once in a while but eventually you should come back and win. Getting coupon returns is one game which the client is delighted to have you win.

The fisherman ad with the headline "To men who want to quit work some day" was reproduced years later in a book by Julian Watkins entitled "The 100 Greatest Advertisements." The ad was the forerunner of a long series of successful ads with retirement income headlines and pictures of men and women having fun while enjoying a guaranteed income for the rest of their lives. That is a campaign I like to think about. Because it has been successful. Because it has done a lot of good by inducing people to make provision for their future years. Not long ago Russ Noyes, Advertising Manager of Phoenix Mutual, afforded me the pleasure of reading a number of letters from Phoenix Mutual policy holders who have retired. They were enthusiastic about the Phoenix Mutual Plan. And they seemed to be enjoying life. I recall the heartfelt comment of one woman in her eighties. She said, "God bless Phoenix Mutual!"

10

How to Write Headlines

O NE WAY to write headlines is to build them around
TESTED KEY WORDS. In the headlines listed below,
the key words are printed in bold letters so that you can pick
them out at a glance. You can take any of these key words that
seem appropriate and build headlines around them. For example, if you have a brand new product or service, you can start
your headline with the word "ANNOUNCING," as follows:

ANNOUNCING NEW FICTION WRITING COURSE
ANNOUNCING A GREAT NEW SELECTION OF
KODAK HOME-MOVIE CAMERAS
GULF **ANNOUNCES** A COMPLETELY NEW AND
DIFFERENT GASOLINE

Other words that give a news flavor to your message are
printed in bold letters in the following headlines. You need not
print the words in bold type in your headlines.

INTRODUCING SALONETTE FURS
PRESENTING NEW 36″ TALL PRIMA BALLERINA
DOLL
TODAY'S DU PONT SPONGE WITH THE LIVELY
MOP-UP ACTION
MODERN GIFT FROM OLD MEXICO

Of course, if desired, you can simply use the word NEW. Here are sample headlines:

NEW LEMON BLOSSOM PIE

NEW RECORD-BREAKING TOP OCTANE SKY CHIEF GASOLINE

NEW! GOLF CLUBS SPECIALLY SIZED FOR YOUNGSTERS

NEW THIN-STRAND SPAGHETTI WITH TENDER BEEFY MEATBALLS—BY FRANCO-AMERICAN

Another word that has a news flavor is NOW. Examples:

NOW $2500 OF TERM LIFE INSURANCE FOR ONLY $1.90 A MONTH

NOW SLEEP UNDER NEW WARMTH . . . NEW BEAUTY!

NOW YOU CAN EAT LIKE A KING—IN BRITAIN

NOW A NEW WAY TO MAKE A LOW-CALORIE BACARDI DAIQUIRI

The words "how," "how I," "how you" and "how to" are excellent for beginning headlines:

HOW CAN THESE MAGNIFICENT NATURE GUIDES BE SOLD AT ONLY $1 EACH?

HOW PEPPERIDGE FARM BREAD HELPS YOU KEEP THAT RADIANT LOOK

HOW I IMPROVED MY MEMORY IN ONE EVENING

HOW I STARTED A NEW LIFE WITH $6

HOW YOU CAN BECOME POPULAR

HOW TO MAKE YOUR LIVING IN FOUR HOURS A DAY

HOW TO READ A WHISKY LABEL

HOW TO KEEP YOUR HUSBAND HOME . . . AND HAPPY

HOW TO GET RID OF AN INFERIORITY COMPLEX

You can begin a headline by naming the group of people you wish to reach. Examples:

TO CAR OWNERS WHO WANT TO CUT GASOLINE BILLS

TO THE MAN WHO IS 35 AND DISSATISFIED

TO A $5000 MAN WHO WOULD LIKE TO BE MAKING $10,000

GIRLS! . . . WANT QUICK CURLS?

TO MEN WHO WANT TO QUIT WORK SOME DAY

TO YOUNG MEN WHO WANT TO GET AHEAD

SPORTSMEN! . . . IMPROVE YOUR SHOOTING SKILL

ADVICE TO WIVES WHOSE HUSBANDS DON'T SAVE MONEY

You can begin your headline with the word "Why." For example:

WHY RYBUTOL CAN MAKE YOU FEEL PEPPIER

WHY SENATOR ADAMS READS *THE READER'S DIGEST*

WHY 20,000,000 FAMILIES SAVE S&H GREEN STAMPS

You can start your headline with the word "You" or "Yours."

YOU CAN LIVE LIKE THIS IN PUERTO RICO TODAY

YOU CAN WASH AND DRY THIS JACKET AUTOMATICALLY IN THE BENDIX DUOMATIC

YOU TIDY YOUR BED IN JUST 20 SECONDS . . . PACIFIC CONTOUR SHEETS

YOURS FOR ONLY 10¢ . . . 9 OF THE WORLD'S GREATEST MUSICAL TREASURES

Listed below are other key words which have been used in successful headlines:

THIS IS THE TIRE WITH BUILT-IN PEACE OF MIND

THIS IS THE WONDERFUL READING LAMP THAT BLENDS FASHION AND FUNCTION BEAUTIFULLY

THIS 49¢ STORM WINDOW PROTECTS YOUR FAMILY ALL WINTER

WHAT'S WRONG WITH THIS PICTURE?

PUT YOURSELF IN THIS PICTURE

FREE YOUR CHOICE OF ANY OF THESE 12″ HIGH FIDELITY COLUMBIA RECORDS

FREE TO NEW MEMBERS OF THE AROUND-THE-WORLD SHOPPERS CLUB

FREE AFRICAN VIOLET BOOKLET

FREE PLATO AND ARISTOTLE

FOUR WAYS TO WRITE TIMELY HEADLINES

If you will go through a series of ad readership tests covering a year or more, you will notice the high readership of *timely* ads, namely, Christmas gift ads, Mother's Day ads, etc.

This high reading of timely ads confirms the results of other tests. For example, coupon returns show the value of a timely message. An ad featuring Christmas gift wraps brought a record number of requests for a booklet entitled, "33 Secrets of Gift Wrapping." Department stores find that timely ads bring more people into the store. Mail order advertisers who use catalogs find that it often pays to send out special seasonal supplements. Editors of magazines and newspapers find that timely articles get better than average reading. Special event broadcasts get more people to tune in.

There is no question about the value of timeliness. It can

win increased attention for your message. The question is HOW do you make your advertising timely? And HOW OFTEN during a twelve-month period can you cash in on a timely appeal? Listed below are four ways to make ads timely.

1. *Conventional Holidays.* These are the well-known holidays you are not likely to forget. They come every year but their appeal never seems to wear out.

New Year's Day	Father's Day
Lincoln's Birthday	Independence Day
Valentine's Day	Labor Day
Washington's Birthday	Columbus Day
Easter	Hallowe'en
Mother's Day	Thanksgiving Day
Memorial Day	Christmas

You can build a special drive around a holiday. For example, Schenley Distillers scheduled a special Labor Day drive, featuring three products for the three-day week-end with the theme "For your coming three-day week-end, here are three ways to enjoy Schenley elegance."

Or you can simply mention the holiday in addition to your regular basic theme. For example, A&P Stores featured low prices as usual before Labor Day, but added this headline: "Timed for the 3-day holiday . . . Value-packed holiday buys!"

If you want a complete list of holidays, write to the Chamber of Commerce of the United States, Washington, D.C., and ask for the booklet entitled, "Special Days, Weeks and Months." The booklet lists over 350 business promotion events, legal holidays, and religious observances.

2. *Special Events.* Perhaps a new ship is about to be launched or is about to start on her maiden voyage. Is your product on

board? Maybe you can build an ad around this. Perhaps a new bridge or highway or airfield or hotel is being opened to the public. Maybe you can feature it.

Perhaps you can tie in with the centennial celebration of some city or state. Also there are such events as Boy Scout Week, Fire Prevention Week, Armed Forces Day, and even Doughnut Week. Some of these may sound a little synthetic, but they do give you a hook to hang a headline on. And don't forget Election Day and Graduation Day.

3. *Seasons.* Here are some typical headlines based on the seasonal appeal.

SPRINGTIME IS PICTURE TIME (Kodak)

YOUR SUMMER HOME IS READY FOR USE (U. S. Surplus Homes)

SAVE IN AUGUST ON REXAL DRUG PRODUCTS

IT'S ANTI-FREEZE WEEK AT DU PONT "ZERONE" AND "ZEREX" DEALERS

If you are looking for a simple way to give your ad a seasonal flavor, you can begin your headline with one of the following time-tested phrases: "This spring" . . . "This summer" . . . "This fall" . . . "This winter."

4. *Feature the Year.* We ran a copy test for a bank. Seven all-type ads with different headlines were tested. One of these ads featured the *year* in the headline and this ad was the winner.

Eight newspaper ads for G. E. Bulbs were tested with a hidden offer. The ad that pulled the most replies had the headline "Why G. E. Bulbs Give More Light *This Year.*" This headline is really a dandy because G. E. engineers are always producing bulbs that give more light with less current. Therefore this headline can be used anytime, any year.

Another headline with this same timeless but timely quality

is "Here is the Perfect Gift for This Moment in the World" written by BBDO Copy Group Head, Carl Spier, for the Revised Standard Version of the Bible. The fact is that ever since most of us can remember, the world has been experiencing a series of crises which make Bible reading appropriate at *any time.* Therefore you don't have to worry about long closing dates with this headline. If today's crisis is solved, there will be another crisis coming up three months from now that will give timeliness to the headline "Here is the Perfect Gift for This Moment in the World."

Timely hint: Put under the blotter on your desk a list of holidays and the next time you have to get up a new ad, take a look at the list and maybe you will think of a timely idea.

HOW TO ATTRACT PROSPECTS

Two insurance advertisements were run in magazines. Both ads contained a sales talk for a retirement income plan and a coupon offering a booklet. One ad had a so-called "rifle bullet" headline which was aimed directly at *prospects.* The other ad had a so-called "shotgun" headline which scattered its effect over a broad area. Here are the headlines of the ads:

1. HOW A MAN OF 40 CAN RETIRE IN 15 YEARS ("rifle bullet" headline)

2. GET A VACATION WITH PAY! ("shotgun" headline)

These ads were tested by three different methods, as follows:

1. By readership reports.

2. By counting coupon returns.

3. By adding up the sales made by salesmen calling on people who mailed in coupons.

Experience shows that the results of method number 2 and method number 3 frequently agree—that is, the ads that bring the most coupons also bring the most sales. The rare exception occurs when a free offer is prominently featured in one ad and subordinated in another ad. In the case of the ad which features the free offer, it may bring more replies, but when salesmen call they find that many of these people are curiosity seekers and not real prospects. Experienced copy testers use the *same subordinated offer* in all ads tested so that the coupon returns (or inquiries from a hidden offer) will be a true indication of the selling power of an ad.

But how well do *readership* tests agree with sales tests? Experience shows that readership tests *sometimes agree and sometimes disagree* with sales tests. In the above mentioned headline test, there was *disagreement*. The ad that got the higher readership got fewer coupons and sales. And the ad that did poorly on readership did well on coupons and sales.

Can you guess which ad is which? Glance back at the two headlines. Once you know the answer, the reasons for the disagreement between readership results and sales results will seem obvious.

The answer is that the winner on coupons and sales was **ad number one** with the headline: "How a man of 40 can retire in 15 years."

Why did this headline win?

1. Because the headline states clearly what is being sold in the copy. There is no let down in interest when the reader gets into the copy.

2. Because the headline appeals to men. And men are the chief buyers of retirement income plans.

3. Because the headline appeals to men in the age bracket when most retirement income plans are started, namely age 35 to 45.

Why did this headline do poorly on *readership*? For the very same reasons. It is a *selective* headline. It did not appeal to women. It did not appeal to very young men or to old men. It eliminated extraneous readership. It appealed only to *prospects*.

It selected just those readers who wanted to read about retirement incomes and who could be induced to send for a booklet containing further information. It is a rifle bullet headline, not a shotgun headline.

Now let us look at the other headline, namely, "Get a vacation with pay." Why did this headline do well on readership and poorly on coupons and sales?

Because it attracts a broad audience but the *wrong audience*. It attempts to stop everybody, men and women, old and young, with the promise of a vacation with pay. Consequently a lot of people read the copy (or *part* of the copy) and the ad got a high readership rating. But when these people read the copy, they discovered that the ad did not actually offer a vacation with pay. Instead it offered a retirement income for which you have to pay money and which does not begin until fifteen years hence.

As a result, only a small proportion of the people who had been drawn into the copy by the vacation promise in the headline were sufficiently interested to mail the coupon. The headline attracted a big group, but not the retirement income buying group. It is a shotgun headline, not a rifle bullet headline.

Moral: If you want your advertising to produce SALES, do not (in your eagerness to attract a big audience) use a headline which fails to attract the very people who will buy your product. Use a headline that SELECTS PROSPECTS.

PICTURES THAT ATTRACT PROSPECTS

In Chapter 8 it was pointed out that in ads for General Electric Bulbs a picture of a woman *putting a bulb into a lamp* pulled better than a *baby picture*. In other words, a picture that was related to the product and which therefore attracted *prospects* was better than a nonrelated picture which failed to attract prospects.

What kind of pictures should you use in order to make your advertising attract prospects and produce sales? Here are three kinds of pictures that work well:

1. Picture of the product itself
2. Picture of the product in use
3. Picture of the reward of using the product

When should you use a picture of the product itself? Answer: When the product itself is *interesting*. For example, in the advertising of hunting rifles, it was found that one of the best-pulling illustrations was a picture of the hunting rifle itself. Sportsman like to look at pictures of rifles. The same applies to camping equipment, boats, clothes, clocks, automobiles, houses, and other products which are interesting in themselves.

On the other hand, in a life insurance ad, it was found that a picture of a life insurance policy did not pull as well as other types of illustrations. And in a test of illustrations for automobile anti-freeze, it was found that a picture of a can of anti-freeze did not pull as well as a picture of a service station man pouring anti-freeze into the radiator of a snow-covered car.

Mail order advertisers are great believers in pictures of the product itself. A mail order advertiser selling paratroop boots showed a picture of the boots. A mail order advertiser selling binoculars showed a picture of binoculars. Book club advertisers show pictures of books. The Sears-Roebuck catalogue is full of pictures of the products themselves.

When do you show the *product in use*? In advertising furniture enamel, a number of different pictures were tested and the best-pulling illustration was a picture of a woman painting a chair. In advertising car polish, a number of pictures were tested and the best puller was a picture of a man polishing a car. Mail order advertisers selling courses in drawing have found that a picture of an artist sketching a beautiful model is effective. In advertising an air conditioning device it was found that a bedroom scene showing a woman asleep with a smile on her face and with her bed near an air conditioning machine was effective. This picture is really a combination of two types of pictures, namely (1) Product in use, and (2) The reward of using the product.

When do you show the *reward of using the product?* Here are some examples. In retirement income advertising, the best pictures are those that show happy, retired people enjoying life. In a test of ads for a hair wave set, a picture of a smiling girl with curls was better than a picture of a girl with straight hair. In a test of a health food, a picture of a smiling, healthy man, who was happy because he had used the product, pulled better than a picture of a sour-looking chap who needed to use the product. In a mail order course for a women's school of nursing, the most effective picture was a photo of a pretty, smiling girl wearing a nurse's cap. Mail order garden seed people find that pictures of beautiful flowers pull better than pictures of seeds.

Naturally, the selection of the right picture to advertise *your product* requires judgment. . . . judgment plus any testing you are able to do. Sometimes you will find that there are several types of pictures that work well. This gives *variety* to your campaign. Sometimes you can do better by using ads without pictures—namely, all-type ads. This permits you to use a longer sales talk. The main thing is to avoid the use of pictures that are too far fetched and too clever. I saw an ad for an airline in which the main illustration was a picture of a *camera.* Naturally, this picture would stop more camera prospects than prospects for airline tickets. And, believe it or not, not long after that I saw a camera ad illustrated with a big picture of an *airliner.*

HOW TO MAKE YOUR CLIENT FAMOUS

Seven advertising appeals for a new household product were tested by running seven newspaper ads. Each ad featured a different appeal in the headline, such as:

1. Works faster
2. Costs less
3. Made by (name of manufacturer)
4. Contains (name of scientific ingredient)

Each ad had a keyed offer in the last paragraph. The ads were tested in three cities.

Before the test was run I thought, "The weakest ad is the one that features the manufacturer's name in the headline. That headline is dull. The other headlines are exciting!"

Imagine my surprise when I discovered that the ad "Made by (name of manufacturer)" was the winner in all three cities!

This is not an isolated case. The same thing later happened in other copy tests. The name of a well-known manufacturer in the headline has more effect on readers than some of the fancy and ingenious headlines which I, as a copy writer, like to dream up.

I used to think I could find in my head (or in the dictionary) some words that are more exciting than Du Pont or General Electric. But apparently I was wrong.

As a writer, I hated to be saddled with the necessity of dragging into my imaginative flights such dull words as the name of the maker of the product. It was like trying to jump over a fence with a ball and chain on my foot. However, due to the results of tests, I am now convinced that a famous manufacturer's name can be a lift instead of a let-down.

If this is so, I wonder *why* it is so? Perhaps readers react as follows:

1. If the headline says the product works faster, *it may or*

may not be true. If the headline says the product contains a scientific ingredient, *it may or may not be important.*

2. On the other hand, if the headline says the product is made by Du Pont or General Electric, *it's got to be true.* And the product *must be good.*

In addition to increasing believability and confidence, the manufacturer's name in the headline has another advantage. It gets the name high up on the page where readers cannot miss it. It helps to make famous names even more famous. Readership tests show that readers frequently fail to read the manufacturer's logotype at the bottom of an ad.

Here is another advantage. If you put the manufacturer's name at the top of the ad, you can often omit it from the bottom of the ad. This makes your ad look more like *editorial material.* This gets higher readership for your copy.

Incidentally, the making of ads that look like editorial material, is a technique which has grown in recent years. Ads are made to look like stories, like articles, like cartoons, like comics, like special features. Readership studies and inquiry tests have shown that ads that do not look like ads can be very effective.

Radio and TV writers have developed to a fine art the technique of starting a commercial in a manner that makes it sound like something other than advertising. For example, here are the opening lines from a beer commercial that starts off like entertainment:

"Here is Guy Lombardo and his orchestra. (Music and singing) . . . I want a girl, just like the girl—"

At this point you expect to hear the familiar words "that married dear old dad." Instead you hear the words, "that's in the Rheingold ads."

During an election year, the editorial flavor at the beginning of a commercial was increased by using the line: "It's the year to vote! So vote in the year's second biggest election. Vote for Miss Rheingold!"

This editorial technique in broadcasting has the advantage that it *gets you started listening,* just as a printed ad, in editorial style, *gets you started reading.*

If you print the advertiser's name in the headline, does it mean that you have to drop the time-tested principles of featuring news, self-interest, low price, etc.? No. Here are ad headlines that combine the advertiser's name with proven appeals.

B. F. GOODRICH . . . FIRST IN TUBELESS . . . BRINGS YOU THE POWER TIRES FOR TODAY'S POWER CARS

A MAN FEELS GOOD WHEN HE'S INSURED
IN NEW ENGLAND MUTUAL LIFE

Here are some headlines written two ways, (a) without the advertiser's name, and (b) with the advertiser's name. Note how version (b) carries more conviction.

(a) WASH YOUR CLOTHES WHITER
WITH DOUBLE ACTION
(b) G. E. WASHES YOUR CLOTHES WHITER
WITH DOUBLE ACTION

(a) YOU GET A WRITTEN GUARANTEE THAT
THIS BURNER SAVES OIL
(b) G. E. GIVES YOU A WRITTEN GUARANTEE
THAT THIS BURNER SAVES OIL

Here are typical headlines which could have contained the advertiser's name but didn't.

1. BRINGS OUT THE BEST IN A MAN
(This could have been written: *"How Blank* brings out the best in a man")

2. NOW: HOSPITAL AND SURGICAL PROTECTION
   FOR PEOPLE 60 TO 70 YEARS OLD GUARANTEED
   CONTINUABLE FOR LIFE

(This headline could have ended with the phrase "continuable
for life *by Blank*")

If you will look through current magazines, you will find many
cases where the manufacturer's name could have been lifted
from the bottom of the ad to the top of the ad.

You may say, "But my client's name is not famous. Putting
his name into headlines will add words without adding pulling
power."

Answer: Putting his name into headlines is a quick way to
make him famous.

11

Ten Ways to Write the First Paragraph

AFTER YOU have stopped people with your headline or your
illustration, what do you do next? How do you *hold* their
attention?

Many readers or listeners are lost by a poorly worded first
sentence—or by a wrong construction of the first paragraph.
How do you avoid this? How do you achieve a successful transi-
tion from "stopper" to sales talk? Described below are ten
methods that have proved successful.

1. CONTINUE THE THOUGHT IN THE HEADLINE

One successful method of holding people's attention is to
let your opening paragraph or paragraphs be an enlargement and
further development of the idea expressed in your headline. If
you stopped a prospect with a certain interrupting idea, you
are not likely to lose him if you give him *more of the same.*

Here is how Claude Hopkins, in his historic series of ads for
Pepsodent, continued in his opening paragraphs the thought he
had originally expressed in his headline:

(Headline) FILM—THE ROBBER OF ALL TOOTH
BEAUTY. LEARN HOW MILLIONS NOW COMBAT IT

(1st Paragraph) *That cloudy coat on teeth is film. At first the
film is viscous—you can feel it now.*

(2nd Paragraph) *That film is clinging. No ordinary tooth-*

144

paste effectively combats it. So, in old-way brushing, much of it clings and stays. Food stains, etc., discolor it, then it forms dingy coats. That is why so many teeth are clouded.

Here is how an ad for Sucaryl noncaloric sweetener uses the same method:

(Headline) YOU CAN SAVE A LOT OF CALORIES
BY SWEETENING WITH SUCARYL

(1st Paragraph) *Sucaryl makes it easy for you to watch your weight . . . by giving you all sugar's sweetness, without a single calorie . . . and no bitterness or aftertaste.*

(Headline) NEW, IMPROVED G.E. PORTABLE MIXER
AT A NEW LOW PRICE . . . $17.95

(1st Paragraph) *Powerful enough to do all mixing jobs, yet weighs less than 3 pounds! Truly portable, so that you take it to the food instead of lugging food to the mixer.*

2. QUOTE AN AUTHORITY

Vic Schwab in his classic ad which started Dale Carnegie's book on the road to fame held the reader's interest in the first paragraph by using an appropriate quotation from a well-known authority.

(Headline) HOW TO WIN FRIENDS
AND INFLUENCE PEOPLE

(1st *Paragraph*) *John D. Rockefeller, Sr., once said: "The ability to deal with people is as purchasable a commodity as sugar or coffee. And I will pay more for that ability than any other under the sun."*

If for some reason you do not wish to name the authority you are quoting, you can use some such phrase as "a well-known authority said." Here is how this method was handled in a famous ad for Instant Postum. The idea for the ad was conceived by Raymond Rubicam.

(Headline) WHY MEN CRACK

(1st Paragraph) *An authority of international standing recently wrote: "You have overeaten and plugged your organs with moderate stimulants, the worst of which are not only alcohol and tobacco, but caffeine and sugar." . . . He was talking to men who crack physically in the race for success.*

Here is how a successful mail order ad held readers in an entertaining manner by quoting *several* authorities:

(Headline) THE SECRET OF MENTAL POWER

(1st Paragraph) *Mark Twain once said that the average man didn't make much use of his head except for the purpose of keeping his necktie from slipping off.*

(2nd Paragraph) *And Prof. William James claimed that the average man uses only about a tenth part of his brain.*

(3rd Paragraph) *And Thomas Edison stated emphatically that most men never amount to much because they don't think.*

(4th Paragraph) *How about you? Etc. . . etc.*

Note: Paragraphs 1, 2 and 3 could have been put into a *single paragraph* but the copy writer wisely used three *short* paragraphs for *easy reading.*

3. CHALLENGE THE READER

In several of his most successful ads for the Alexander Hamilton Institute, Bruce Barton used a reverse twist in his opening paragraphs. Instead of saying "Come on, everybody," he held up a warning finger and said in effect, "Wait a minute. Maybe you aren't good enough to measure up to this proposition!"

One of these ads was discussed in detail in Chapter 7. Here is the opening:

(Headline) A WONDERFUL TWO YEARS' TRIP
AT FULL PAY—BUT ONLY MEN WITH
IMAGINATION CAN TAKE IT

(1st Paragraph) *About one man in ten will be appealed to by
this page. The other nine will be hard workers, earnest, ambitious in their way, but to them a coupon is a coupon; a book
is a book; a Course is a Course. The one man in ten has imagination.*

(2nd Paragraph) *And imagination rules the world.*

Another successful Institute ad by Barton began with the
same twist. The ad opened with a description of the free book
as follows: "This book may not be intended for you—but thousands found in it what they were seeking."

And another of Barton's Institute ads which was repeated for
years because of its coupon pulling power began like this:

(Headline) MEN WHO "KNOW IT ALL" ARE NOT
INVITED TO READ THIS PAGE

(Opening Paragraphs) *Among the men enrolled in the Alexander Hamilton Institute there are more than 24,000 presidents
and business heads. The Institute welcomes inquiries from such
men, but this particular page is not addressed to them.*

*Neither is it for the wise young man who is perfectly satisfied
with himself and his business equipment; who knows that the
only reason he is not paid twice as much is because he has never
been "given a chance."*

Some successful recruiting ads prepared by BBDO, for the
U.S. Navy began with the same thought, namely, "the Navy is
wonderful, but can you qualify?"

A successful campaign for Liberty Mutual car insurance used
the same restrictive technique. The ads pointed out that the

benefits of the Liberty Mutual plan are denied to accident-prone car drivers who cause increases in the cost of car insurance. Here is a sample:

(Headline) IF YOU ARE A CAREFUL DRIVER YOU
CAN SAVE MONEY ON CAR INSURANCE

(1st Paragraph) *If you are a careful driver, we believe you are entitled to car insurance at lower cost. With us, you do not have to pay the same price for automobile insurance as dangerous, reckless drivers. Here is the way our plan works: Selected drivers, hence fewer accidents and fewer losses—savings returned to you.*

A cartoonist illustrated in a laughable way the results of one dire instance of the application of the restrictive technique. Two men were shown talking. One looked sad:

(1st Man): *"What's wrong, Joe?"*

(Sad-Looking Man) *"I've just been 'blackballed' by the Book-of-the-Month Club!"*

Mark Twain told the following story illustrating the effectiveness of the restrictive technique in advertising. He said, in effect:

A traveling vaudeville show was operated by a practical psychologist. He put on the show for two nights at each town he visited. On the first night, he put in front of the theatre a big sign which read "For Men Only." He attracted a big crowd. On the second night he attracted another big crowd by putting up a sign "For Women Only."

4. LET THE MANUFACTURER SPEAK

Write your copy so that the maker of the product talks directly to the prospect, in a sort of one-way conversation. This technique was used by J. Stirling Getchell in his well-remembered campaign for Plymouth cars.

(Headline) "LOOK AT ALL THREE! . . . BUT DON'T
BUY ANY LOW-PRICED CAR UNTIL YOU'VE
DRIVEN THE NEW PLYMOUTH
WITH FLOATING POWER
(Subhead) A STATEMENT BY WALTER P. CHRYSLER
(1st Paragraph) *Thousands of people have been waiting ex-
pectantly until today before buying a new car. I hope that you
are one of them.*

(2nd Paragraph) *Now that the new low-priced cars are here
(including the new Plymouth which will be shown on Saturday)
I urge you to carefully* compare *values.*

(3rd Paragraph) *This is the time for you to "shop" and buy
wisely.* Don't make a deposit on any automobile until you've
actually had a demonstration.

Here are additional examples:

(Headline) OLD JIM YOUNG'S
MOUNTAIN-GROWN APPLES
(Subhead) EVERY BITE CRACKLES AND
THE JUICE RUNS DOWN YOUR LIPS
(Opening Paragraphs) *Dear Reader—About fifteen years ago,
out here in New Mexico, my Pappy bought himself an aban-
doned homestead, in a little valley 6000 feet up in the Jemez
Mountains.*

*When folks first saw it they nearly died laughing. "What're
you going to raise, Pappy," they said, "rattlesnakes or gophers?"*

CRAZY—LIKE A FOX
*But riding through the place before he bought it, Pappy had
noticed an old neglected apple tree, with lots of apples on it.*

(Headline) JUMBO PRUNES—SPECIAL
INTRODUCTORY OFFER

(1st Paragraph) *Send me two $1 bills (or check or money order for the same amount) and I will send you my 2¼-pound box of Jumbo Prunes, including a generous sample of my ranch-made Sweets, giant California Apricots, fresh Dates and honey-sweet white Figs.*

You will recall the successful mail order ad (described in Chapter 2) that used this same "me to you" technique.

(Headline) GIVE ME 5 DAYS AND I'LL GIVE
YOU A MAGNETIC PERSONALITY
(Opening Paragraphs) *I can so magnetize your personality that people will be drawn to you at once, irresistibly.*

I can make you a magnet of human attraction so that you are popular everywhere, in any society.

(Headline) THEY THOUGHT I WAS CRAZY TO
SHIP LIVE MAINE LOBSTERS AS FAR AS
1800 MILES FROM THE OCEAN
(Subhead) BUT I HAVE ALREADY SHIPPED 18,685 OF THEM
AND MY CUSTOMERS ARE DELIGHTED!
(1st Paragraph) *When I began talking about shipping live Maine lobsters direct to the homes of seafood lovers all over the country—many of my friends here shook their heads. Veteran lobstermen told me I was crazy. Whoever heard of selling live lobsters by mail? For generations, lobsters had been sold only through the traditional channels of trade—from lobsterman to distributor to wholesaler to retailer to consumer. Me and my new-fangled notions! Down Easterners, of course are strong for tradition. I am too, but I also believe in Yankee ingenuity.*

5. GIVE FREE INFORMATION
One way to hold people's attention is to start right in at the beginning by giving *free information.* In other words give the

reader something of value in exchange for his time.

One of the best-read campaigns of all time uses this technique. It is the informative, health-promoting series of ads published by the Metropolitan Life Insurance Company. Here is a sample:

(Headline) HERE'S A GOOD WAY TO
START A GOOD DAY

(Opening Paragraphs) *Nutrition authorities say that both adults and children miss many helpful benefits if they fail to eat a good breakfast.*

Without breakfast, mid-morning fatigue sometimes occurs along with irritability and difficulty in concentrating on work or studies.

What is a good breakfast? It should supply 25 to 33 per cent of the vital nutrients needed for the day. It should include fruit, bread made from whole grain or enriched flour; cereal or eggs, meat or fish; and milk either to drink or use on cereal or in a cooked dish.

Here are more examples:

(Headline) DOGS AND "DOG DAYS"
(Subhead) Hints on hot-weather care for your dog—
By Dr. John Bernotavicz,
Director, Gaines Research Kennels

(1st Paragraph) *During July and August, the Dog Star, Sirius, is the last star to disappear from the heavens at daybreak. Hence the name "dog days." It has little to do with the mad dogs who are supposed to "go out in the midday sun." In fact, most dogs have a knack for taking life easy in hot weather. A shady spot for snoozing, cool drinking water, proper feeding, and protection against insects will see your dog through summer's hottest and muggiest days in relative comfort.*

(Headline) THE BETTER WAY TO BAKE FISH
(1st Paragraph) *Reynolds Wrap shines especially in Lenten meal-making. Broil fish on a "tray" made of foil, or line the broiler pan, and avoid scouring. Line casseroles and they stay clean. And for baking fish . . . just wrap completely in Reynolds Wrap. You seal in flavor, avoid cooking odor—and have no pan to wash! Perfect for whole stuffed fish, or fresh or frozen fillets.*

Other examples of ads that hold readers' attention by giving information of value are:

1. The Armstrong Linoleum ads that give women ideas for home decoration by featuring 4-color pictures of attractive home interiors.

2. The General Mills Betty Crocker recipe ads that give women instructions for preparing the attractive dishes that are shown in the 4-color illustrations.

6. START WITH A TESTIMONIAL

This is the method that was used in the series of newspaper ads that years ago started Rinso on the road to sales leadership.

(Headline) WHO ELSE WANTS A WHITER WASH—
WITH NO HARD WORK?
(1st Paragraph) *"Rinso soaks everything clean; so I have no more boiling to do, no hard rubbing on a washboard. Little wonder that my clothes last a lot longer. And Rinso isn't hard on my hands either."* Mrs. Geo. N. Tapp; 13 Haviland St., Boston, Mass.

Below are more examples of successful ads that start with testimonials:

(Headline) WHY WALL STREET JOURNAL
READERS LIVE BETTER
(Subhead) BY A SUBSCRIBER

(Opening Paragraphs) *I work in a large city. Over a period of time I noticed that men who read The Wall Street Journal are better dressed, drive better cars, have better homes and eat in better restaurants.*

I said to myself, "Which came first, the hen or the egg? Do they read The Journal because they have more money, or do they have more money because they read The Journal?"

(Headline) THERE'S COLD CREAM NOW IN CAMAY
(1st Paragraph) *Mrs. Robert Steller, an exquisite new Camay Bride says, "New Camay with cold cream is so luxurious! I love it! It's the only beauty soap for me."*

(Headline) LOOK LOVELIER IN TEN DAYS
(1st Paragraph) *Dry, blemished skin: "My doctor recommended Noxzema for my blemishes," says Diana Millay, Rye, N.Y. "It helped my skin look smoother, fresher!"*
(2nd Paragraph) *"Make-up troubles disappeared after Noxzema helped heal my blemishes!" says Linda Rand, Fowlerville, Mich. "My skin looks so much nicer."*

(Headline) $95 AN HOUR
(1st Paragraph) *"Every hour I spent on my I.C.S. course has been worth $95 to me! My position, my $7000 a year income, my home, my family's happiness—I owe it all to spare time training with International Correspondence Schools!"*
(2nd Paragraph) *Every mail brings letters from some of the 5,918,632 I.C.S. students telling of promotions and pay raises —rewards of spare-time study.*

(Headline) RACING'S MOST COVETED AWARD AGAIN
WON WITH CHAMPION SPARK PLUGS
(1st Paragraph) *"When you're up against the best drivers*

and cars in the nation, you want spark plugs that stay with you,"
says Chuck Stevenson, AAA National Racing Champion.

(Headline) HOW DO YOU KNOW YOU CAN'T WRITE?

(1st Paragraph) *Sells first story at 60 . . . "Since I am crowd-*
ing three-score, my objective in taking the N.I.A. Course was
not to become a professional writer. However, while still taking
the course, I sent an article to St. Joseph's Magazine. It was
immediately accepted. 'Our Navy' accepted others. All thanks
to N.I.A."—Albert M. Hinman, East Silver Street, Tucson,
Arizona.

7. GIVE SPECIFICATIONS OF THE PRODUCT

This method is widely used by mail order advertisers and department store advertisers. Here are examples:

(Headline) OLD SOUTHERN FRUIT CAKE OF
LEGENDARY GOODNESS

(1st Paragraph) *Made by a secret recipe cherished by five*
generations in one family, Old Southern Fruitcake is the
gourmet's delight . . . rich with rare and exotic fruit . . . chock-
ful of plump jumbo pecans, almonds and Tennessee black
walnuts . . . mellow with a secret formula blend of rare spices
. . . all captured in a moist but light cake texture of melt-in-the-
mouth goodness.

(Headline) KODASCOPE ROYAL 16MM PROJECTOR

(1st Paragraph) *Powerful 750-watt lamp—for breath-taking*
screen brilliance. (Accepts 1000-watt lamp for auditorium show-
ings, too!) . . . Ultrafast f/1.6 lens with special element that
assures over-all image sharpness . . . Simple, positive controls,
handily located. Geared reel arms, automatic rewind . . . Re-
versing control for comic effect or editing convenience . . .

built-in carrying case—as smart as it is durable . . . Quiet running and lubricated for life!

(Headline) GIBSON GIRL SHIRTWAIST DRESS
(1st Paragraph) *An enchanting dress of fine Cortley "Reflex" cotton, accented with frothy finely pleated jabot and cuffs edged with white lace. Tiny Johnny Collar, self belt and soft skirt of whirling unpressed pleats. Washable, colorfast, crease resistant and preshrunk. Carib blue, sand beige, rogue red or nugget gold. Junior sizes 5 to 15.*

(Headline) PORTABLE 3-SPEED PHONOGRAPH
(1st Paragraph) *Plays 33⅓, 45 and 78-rpm records—7, 10, or 12-inch sizes—one needle, one light tone arm. Gives good performance for such a modest-priced phonograph. Embodies many construction features usually found in much higher priced models. Wonderful for youngsters—easy-to-play—takes a lot of abuse! 1 tube plus rectifier. 4-inch speaker. Strong wood case with interlocked corners. Covered in natural tan kidskin imitation leather with contrasting interior.*

8. USE THE EDITORIAL APPROACH

Here is how the editorial approach was used by Bruce Barton in an advertisement for the Alexander Hamilton Institute:

(Headline) THE GLORY OF THE UPWARD PATH
(Opening Paragraphs) *Two paths begin at the bottom of the hill of life.*

One of them winds about the base, through years of routine and drudgery. Now and then it rises over a knoll representing a little higher plane of living made possible by hard earned progress; but its route is slow and difficult and bordered with monotony.

The other mounts slowly at first, but rapidly afterwards, into positions where every problem is new and stirring, and where the rewards are comfort and travel and freedom from all fear.

Here is another Alexander Hamilton ad which starts with the editorial approach. This one was written by Jim Rorty:

(Headline) WANTED: SAFE MEN FOR
DANGEROUS TIMES

(Opening Paragraphs) *Business today needs, and needs desperately, executives with fresh minds and up-to-date equipment —men who are safe, not in the discarded sense of dodging decisions, but in the modern sense of making them and making them right.*

During the next five very dangerous and exciting years, the new competition will make the fortunes of a lot of such men— and incidentally toss a lot of others on the scrap pile.

Here is the beginning of a famous ad written by Theodore MacManus for Cadillac.

(Headline) THE PENALTY OF LEADERSHIP

(Opening Paragraphs) *In every field of human endeavor, he that is first must perpeutally live in the white light of publicity.*

Whether the leadership be vested in a man or in a manufactured product, emulation and envy are ever at work.

In art, in literature, in music, in industry, the reward and the punishment are always the same.

The reward is widespread recognition; the punishment, fierce denial or detraction.

A newspaper ad signed by Wendell Wilkie (then President of the Commonwealth and Southern Corporation) used the editorial approach in protesting increasing government ownership of utilities.

(Headline) TONIGHT AT MIDNIGHT WE HAND OVER
OUR TENNESSEE ELECTRIC PROPERTIES
AND A $2,800,000 TAX PROBLEM

(Opening Paragraphs) *At midnight tonight, The Commonwealth and Southern Corporation turns over to various public
officials all of its electric properties in the State of Tennessee.*

*We have always believed, and still believe, that the interests
of the public are better served by privately operated utilities
than by publicly operated plants.*

9. USE THE YOU APPROACH

This method consists of talking directly to the prospect and
frequently repeating the words "You" and "Yours." Examples:

(Headline) TO THE MAN WHO IS AFRAID TO LET
HIS DREAM COME TRUE

(Opening Paragraphs) *Years ago you heard of Rolls-Royce—
later you saw one—and a dream formed in your mind . . .
"Some day, when I have the money, I'm going to own that car!"*

*Now you have the money—and you waver. A dozen bogies
buzz about your ears . . . "I can get along with a cheaper car"
. . . "Is Rolls-Royce really worth the price?" . . . "Maybe folks
would think I'm splurging" . . .*

Here is how Bruce Barton used the "You" approach in the
first paragraph of an ad for the Harvard Classics. This ad pulled
eight times as many coupons as had been received from any
previous ad.

(Illustration) Picture of proud-looking woman riding in a
crude wagon

(Headline) THIS IS MARIE ANTOINETTE
RIDING TO HER DEATH

(1st Paragraph) *Do you know her tragic story? Have you read what Burke wrote about the French Revolution—one of the great fascinating books that have made history?*

(Headline) WARNING FROM THE WALL
STREET JOURNAL

(Opening Paragraphs) *This year, you will need to keep up to the minute on news affecting your future and the future of your business.*

Because the reports in The Wall Street Journal come to you daily, you get the fastest possible warning of any new trend that may affect your business and your personal income. You get the facts in time to protect your interests, or to seize quickly a new profit-making opportunity.

10. TELL A STORY

This method has been used in many ads that have become famous. Here is an example taken from a mail order ad for the Roth Memory Course. It was written by the late Wilbur Ruthrauff.

(Headline) HOW I IMPROVED MY MEMORY
IN ONE EVENING

(Subhead) THE AMAZING EXPERIENCE OF VICTOR JONES

(Opening Paragraphs) *"Of course I place you! Mr. Addison Sims of Seattle.*

"If I remember correctly—and I do remember correctly—Mr. Burroughs, the lumberman introduced me to you at the luncheon of the Seattle Rotary Club three years ago in May. This is a pleasure indeed! I haven't laid eyes on you since that day. How is the grain business? How did that merger work out?"

The assurance of this speaker—in the crowded corridor of the Hotel St. Regis—compelled me to look at him.

"He is David M. Roth, the most famous memory expert in the United States," said my friend Kennedy.

The well-known series of Listerine ads frequently uses the story approach. Here is one of the best-remembered of these ads. It was written by Milton Feasley.

(Headline) OFTEN A BRIDESMAID BUT
NEVER A BRIDE

(Opening Paragraphs) *Edna's case was really a pathetic one. Like every woman, her primary ambition was to marry. Most of the girls of her set were married—or about to be. Yet no one possessed more grace or charm or loveliness than she.*

And as her birthdays crept gradually toward that tragic thirty-mark, marriage seemed farther from her life than ever.

She was often a bridesmaid but never a bride.

That's the insidious thing about halitosis (unpleasant breath). You, yourself, rarely know when you have it. And even your closest friends won't tell you.

(Headline) THEY INVENTED A MONEY THAT
CAN'T BE LOST OR STOLEN

(Opening Paragraphs) *For minutes, there was a third person in the bedroom of the sleeping couple from Toronto. When he vanished into the early Florida morning, so had the wife's purse. Yet in scarcely 10 hours—and while the thief still remained un-captured—$1080 of the $1150 he had stolen was back in their hands!*

How was it done? The visitors from Toronto had simply notified the Miami office of American Express. Although the $70 in cash was gone forever, the other $1080 was in the world's safest currency—American Express Travelers Cheques, for which there was an immediate refund.

Chapter 6 tells the incident of the mail order book buyer who wrote to the publisher of Benvenuto Cellini's Autobiography and said "The man who wrote the ad should have written the book!"

Here is a case where the author of the ad *also wrote the book*. Lillian Eichler wrote the *Book of Etiquette* for publisher Doubleday and then wrote a remarkable series of human-interest ads that helped to sell two million copies of the book.

Here is the headline and the opening paragraphs of one of the most famous of these ads. Notice how skillfully the story prepares the reader's mind for a sales talk for the *Book of Etiquette*.

(Headline) AGAIN SHE ORDERS—"A CHICKEN SALAD, PLEASE"

(Opening Paragraphs) *For him she is wearing her new frock. For him she is trying to look her prettiest. If only she can impress him—make him like her—just a little.*

Across the table he smiles at her, proud of her prettiness, glad to notice that others admire. And she smiles back, a bit timidly, a bit self-consciously.

What wonderful poise he has! What complete self-possession! If only she could be so thoroughly at ease.

She pats the folds of her new frock nervously, hoping that he will not notice how embarrassed she is, how uncomfortable. He doesn't—until the waiter comes to their table and stands, with pencil poised, to take the order.

"A chicken salad, please." She hears herself give the order as in a daze. She hears him repeat the order to the waiter, in a rather surprised tone. Why had she ordered that again! This was the third time she had ordered chicken salad while dining with him.

He would think she didn't know how to order a dinner. Well, did she? No. She didn't know how to pronounce those French words on the menu. And she didn't know how to use the table appointments as gracefully as she would have liked; found that she couldn't create conversation—and was actually tongue-tied; was conscious of little crudities which she just knew he must be noticing. She wasn't sure of herself, she didn't know. *And she discovered, as we all do, that there is only one way to have complete poise and ease of manner, and that is to know definitely what to do and say on every occasion.*

For your convenience, the ten ways to start an ad that have been discussed in this chapter, are summarized below:

1. *Continue the thought in the headline.*
2. *Quote an authority.*
3. *Challenge the reader.*
4. *Let the manufacturer speak.*
5. *Give free information.*
6. *Start with a testimonial.*
7. *Give specifications of the product.*
8. *Use the editorial approach.*
9. *Use the YOU approach.*
10. *Tell a story.*

12

How to Write Advertising Copy

L ET US say that you have selected a good selling appeal for your proposition (in accordance with the principles discussed in Chapter 8).

And you have written a headline that will get the attention of prospects (as discussed in Chapter 10).

And you have written a first paragraph that will cause prospects to start reading your ad or listening to your commercial (as outlined in Chapter 11).

Now you are well on your way towards creating a successful advertisement. You have your prospect's attention and interest. What next? . . .

Your are faced with two problems:

1. How do you continue to hold your prospect's interest?
2. How do you sell him?

In some cases you can continue the same style which you used in your opening paragraphs. In other cases you will need to change to a different style.

CONTINUING THE SAME STYLE

The Plymouth ad which was quoted in Chapter 11 is an example of where the style of the opening paragraph is continued throughout the entire ad. You will recall that in the opening paragraph, Walter Chrysler speaks directly to the reader in these words:

Thousands of people have been waiting expectantly until today before buying a new car. I hope that you are one of them.

The ad continues in the same conversational style for nine paragraphs and ends with this paragraph:

Again let me urge you, go and see the new Plymouth with Floating Power on Saturday. Be sure to look at all THREE low-priced cars and don't buy any until you do. That is the way to get the most for your money.

Other cases where you can make your ad a continuation of the opening paragraph are as follows:

1. *Where your first paragraph gives specifications of the product.*

2. *Where your first paragraph uses the YOU approach.*

STORY COPY

If your ad begins with a STORY, you have two choices:

1. *You can switch to a different style of copy after you have completed your story.*

2. *Or you can write your entire ad in the form of a story.*

Here is an example of a classic ad that was written entirely in the form of a story:

(Headline) EVER HEAR THE ONE ABOUT
THE FARMER'S DAUGHTER?

(Copy) *It seems that one day a traveling salesman in a smart new Buick pulled up at the gate where the girl was standing.*

"Nice day," said he, lifting his hat. "Wonderful!" she agreed.

"Nice sort of day to take a nice long automobile ride," he suggested. "Wonderful!" said the farmer's daughter.

"Got a pretty snappy car here," said the traveling salesman.

"Just about the handsomest thing to be seen anywhere!"

Again the girl agreed—"It's wonderful!"

"It's got a swell engine," said the salesman. *"Gets more good out of every drop of gasoline. A Dynaflash straight-eight! You ought to see it travel!"*

"Wonderful!" said the farmer's daughter.

"Darned comfortable car too. Those BuiCoil Springs certainly do make the rough roads behave. Never driven a car that travels smoother."

Said the farmer's daughter: "Just wonderful!"

"And look! Big windows. You can see the country. Why there's 413 more square inches of safety glass in this sedan. It's a treat to travel in a car like this!"

"Wonderful!" agreed the girl.

"Well," said the salesman, *"how about taking a little ride with me?"*

"Look, mister!" said the farmer's daughter. *"Where you been? We've two Buicks in the garage. Want to race to town?"*

A CHANGE IN STYLE

In some cases you will need to change to a different style after you have written your opening paragraph.

For example, if your opening paragraph is a *challenge* to the reader, you will not be able to continue in that vein throughout the entire ad. You have to get into a selling vein sooner or later.

The same applies to ads that begin with an editorial, or with free information, or with a testimonial. These things are excellent beginnings, but it is not easy, for example, to build an entire ad out of testimonials.

The same applies if you open your ad with a quotation from an authority. Here is how Vic Schwab switched from quotation-style to selling-style in his famous ad that was mentioned in Chapter 10.

(Headline) HOW TO WIN FRIENDS
AND INFLUENCE PEOPLE

(Opening Paragraphs) *John D. Rockefeller, Sr. once said:*
"The ability to deal with people is as purchasable a commodity
as sugar or coffee. And I will pay more for that ability than for
any other under the sun."

Wouldn't you suppose every college would conduct practical
courses to develop this "highest priced ability under the sun?"
To our knowledge, none has.

How to develop that ability is the subject of Dale Carnegie's
amazing new book.

A few years ago Chicago University and the United Y.M.C.A.
Schools made a survey to find out the prime interest of adults.
The survey took two years, cost $25,000. It indicated that their
first interest is health, and their second, how to understand
and get along with people; how to make people like you; how
to win others to your way of thinking.

Wouldn't you suppose that after the members of this survey
committee had decided to give such a course, they could readily
have found a practical textbook? They searched diligently, yet
could find none suitable.

The book they were looking for was recently published, and
overnight became a best seller. 36,000 copies were sold in three
days of last week alone. More than 500,000 copies have been
sold to date! It is outselling any other book in America today.

(Author's note: Sales are now over 4 million.)

TELLING THE HISTORY OF THE PRODUCT

One type of copy that can sometimes be used effectively is to
tell a brief history of the product.

At first glance you may feel that an ad which tells the history
of the product is bad because it contains so-called manufactur-

er's copy—that it wrongly stresses the "me" angle instead of rightly stressing the "you" angle.

However, a number of famous and successful ads (including the above ad by Vic Schwab) have contained a history of the product, told in a manner which makes the history a powerful selling device. It all depends on how you do it. Below are examples of how it was done by some of the other masters of advertising copy.

In a toothpaste ad, Claude Hopkins, after describing how film causes tooth decay, told the following story:

. . . So dental investigators started out to find a way to fight film. In this research two methods were discovered. One disintegrates the film at all stages of formation. One removes it without harmful scouring.

Able authorities have proved these methods effective, by many careful tests. A new-style toothpaste was created to apply them daily. The name is Pepsodent. Etc. . . etc.

Here is how Raymond Rubicam used the historical angle in the famous series of Squibb ads featuring the basic theme: "The priceless ingredient of every product is the honor and integrity of its maker."

E. R. Squibb & Sons was founded in 1858 by Dr. Edward R. Squibb, a physician and chemist of high principles and ideals. He was inspired, not by hope of financial gain (for he had money enough for all his needs), but by professional duty and personal honor. His aim was to set a new and higher standard in chemical and pharmaceutical manufacture, by making products of greater purity than had yet been known.

Within three years the Squibb Laboratories had attained a position of leadership. In 1861 the Government of the United States turned confidently to Squibb for products needed for a million men in our Civil War. Etc. . . . etc.

Here is how George Cecil used history to introduce a new ginger ale:

DOWN FROM CANADA CAME TALES
OF A WONDERFUL BEVERAGE

For years and years, visitors to Canada have come back with tales of a wonderful ginger ale. They described its exquisite flavor—they told of drinking it in the Houses of Parliament in Ottawa, in the residence of the Governor-General, and in the Royal Canadian Yacht Club.

Friends would listen and smack their lips and ask if there wasn't some way to purchase it in this country. And the answer was always "No."

Then the Canadian owners were induced to open a selling agency in this country and "Canada Dry," for the first time, was officially brought to the United States. Etc. . . . etc.

Webb Young, famous copy writer, began one of his classic necktie ads with a bit of history.

HAND WOVEN BY THE MOUNTAIN
PEOPLE OF NEW MEXICO
(photo of neckties)

For over 200 years the Spanish people who settled New Mexico have been raising sheep and weaving wool. Their looms and their craft have been handed down from father to son. And the colorful landscape in which these people have-lived and worked has made natural artists of them.

Today I take the lovely fabrics these people weave and have them made up into such stunning ties as are shown here. These are as true reproductions as the modern color camera can get, made direct from the ties. Etc. . . etc.

Note: Julian Watkins, in his book "The 100 Greatest Advertisements" credits this ad with selling more than 26,000 neckties straight from just one page ad in *Life* magazine.

G. Lynn Sumner used the following historical introduction in a famous ad:

IMAGINE HARRY AND ME ADVERTISING OUR PEARS IN FORTUNE!

Out here on the ranch we don't pretend to know much about advertising, and maybe we're foolish spending the price of a tractor for this space; but my brother and I got an idea the other night, and we believe you folks who read Fortune are the kind of folks who'd like to know about it. So here's our story:

We have a beautiful orchard out here in the Rogue River Valley in Oregon, where the soil and the rain and the sun grow the finest pears in the world. Years ago we decided to specialize on Royal Riviera Pears, a rare, delicious variety originally imported from France. And do you know where we sold our first crop? In Paris and London, where the finest hotels and restaurants serve them at about 75 cents each! Etc. . . . etc.

Note: This ad ended with an order blank. It made a remarkable sales record, won an advertising award for the best magazine ad of the year, and started a new industry of selling fruit by mail.

RAPID-FIRE COPY

Two prize fighters faced each other in the center of the ring. After several rounds of sparring, one fighter dropped his guard for a fraction of a second. The other fighter saw the opening and delivered, not just one punch, not just two punches, but a rapid fire of punches with the speed of a locomotive piston.

This same rapid-fire technique can also be used effectively in writing advertising copy. The headline of your ad, if it contains a believable promise to the right audience, will cause your prospect to drop his guard for a fraction of a second. You can then deliver, not just one sales argument, not just two sales arguments, but a rapid fire of sales arguments.

Both the prize fighter and the copy writer are, in a sense, salesmen. The prize fighter tries to sell his opponent the idea of lying down on the canvas. The copy writer tries to sell his prospect the idea of parting with money. Both jobs are difficult.

Here is an example of rapid-fire copy from a successful mail order ad:

COURSE IN SHORTHAND

Shorthand in 6 weeks at home. Low cost. Write 120 words per minute. Age no obstacle. Famous Speedwriting Shorthand System. No signs; no symbols; no machines; uses ABC's. Easy to learn and use. Fast preparation for a position. Nationally used in leading offices and Civil Service; also by executives, writers, speakers, lawyers, scientists, students at college. Over 100,000 taught by mail.

In ads selling books, a table of contents of the book, set in a panel in the ad, helps to sell by the rapid-fire method. For example, here is a panel from the ad "How to Win Friends and Influence People."

THIS IS A BIG BOOK OF 37 CHAPTERS, INCLUDING:
The big secret of dealing with people
Six ways to make people like you instantly
An easy way to become a good conversationalist
A simple way to make a good first impression
How to interest people
Twelve ways to win people to your way of thinking
A sure way of making enemies—and how to avoid it

In ads offering to send a free booklet, the rapid-fire, table-of-contents technique is also helpful. Here is the subhead and copy panel from an ad offering a free booklet on mental power. This ad brought inquiries for only 18¢ each.

GET THIS FREE BOOK IF YOU ARE INTERESTED IN LEARNING:
—*How to think like an arrow*
—*How to compel attention*
—*How to master important problems*
—*How to overcome fear and worry*
—*How to tune up your mental motor*
—*How to originate new ideas*
—*How to out-think the average man*

There are hundreds of examples of rapid-fire copy to be found in mail-order advertising. For example, here is a paragraph from an ad for hunting boots:

Super quality in every way. Single, soft piece of leather forms both vamp and insole. No seams to bind or irritate. Gives you a smooth, flexible construction for greatest comfort. Genuine Canadian hand-sewn vamp. Top grade oil-tanned cowhide uppers, waterproof as leather can be. Genuine crepe rubber sole and heel for sure-footed walking. Leather midsole, heel pad. Full leather gusset repels water. Strong leather laces . . . Pair $13.95.

The next time you write an ad designed to get immediate sales, why not try rapid-fire copy? Get in there and fight. Throw punches fast. Remember that in the long run, your prospect must buy or you must lose your job as an ad writer. You are battling for a purse—*his purse!*

If the comparison between prize fighting and copy writing seems like too savage an analogy, remember this big difference. In prize fighting, only one can win. But in ad writing, if you are selling a good product, both sides can win. Because you confer a benefit on your prospect by inducing him to buy.

POETIC COPY

When I was a boy, my mother read aloud to me from the works of Shakespeare, Marlowe, Robert Burns, Tennyson, and other poets. She tried to instill in me the love she felt for classical literature. She was only partly successful in this endeavor.

At college I wrote some verse for the Annapolis Log, but it was mostly humorous verse. And when I got my first job as a mail order copy writer, I tried to write some poetic copy. But copy chief Ev Grady steered me into more prosaic (and more profitable) channels.

After a year of mail order copy writing I proudly brought home my scrapbook of ads I had written and showed them to my mother. I recall her dismay as she turned the pages and read these rather crude-sounding, mail order headlines:

End dandruff in 48 hours . . . or no cost!
Fat men—new reducing belt takes off 5 inches in 5 days!
60 days ago they called me "Baldy"!
Overnight I stopped being the underdog!

Mother's only comment was: "Don't let your father see this!"
Years later, while listening to the radio I heard this line in a toothpaste commercial:
What is it that's missing, missing, missing *in every other leading toothpaste?*
The repetition of the word "missing" carried me back to my poetry days. Do you recall this line by Robert Burns? "My love is like a red, red rose." The repetition of the word "red" makes the rose seem redder.

Do you recall the scene where Antony was mortally wounded? He turned to Cleopatra (nicknamed "Egypt") and said: "I am dying, Egypt, dying!" The repetition of the word "dying" makes the line more effective.

Hamlet used repetition. He said: "Oh that this, *too, too* solid flesh would melt!"

What a line for a reducing ad!

Then there is the more recent line: "Tramp, tramp, tramp, the boys are marching." The repetition of the word "tramp" helps you to hear their footsteps.

Perhaps the modern copy writer CAN learn something from poetry. In broadcast advertising where you cannot emphasize certain words by putting them in BIG PRINT, it is possible to get emphasis by using the poets' technique of REPETITION.

Another technique that can be borrowed from poetry is the use of *poetic phrases*. For example, do you recall the line written by the poet Keats:

> *Oh for a draft of vintage that hath been*
> *Cooled a long age in the deep-delved earth!*

Keats was ill and in the hospital when he wrote that line and he felt the need of a cooling, refreshing glass of wine. The fact is, if he had simply placed a bottle of wine on his window sill overnight, it would have acquired the proper temperature. But the phrase "cooled a long age" creates the illusion of an especially desirable degree of coolness. And the phrase "in the deep-delved earth" seems to add a unique flavor to the wine.

Speaking of wine, here is some rather poetic copy from a circular mailed by the Sherry Wine and Spirits Company:

CLOS BLANC . . .

For centuries, the good Cisterian Monks who labor in the vineyards of Clos de Vougeot have made it a practice to dedicate a small portion of the vineyard to the production of white wine. You will be delighted with the exquisite finesse and unique bouquet of this collector's item.

MONTRACHET . . .

The tiny bit of soil called "Le Montrachet," whose stonewall gives it the look of a cemetery, produces what many believe to be the greatest white wine on earth. Its eighteen acres yield less than 2000 cases in a good year—nowhere near enough to meet the world demand.

Poetic copy sometimes makes its appearance on restaurant menus. The average restaurant owner simply lists items such as Long Island scallops, chicken curry, hamburger steak, etc. But the Beverly Restaurant in New York described these items on a recent menu as follows:

Hearts of Long Island Scallops delicately sauteed in Meuniere Butter to a golden brown.

Slivers of Young Capon in a taste-tingling India Curry Sauce atop fluffy white rice.

Broiled Chopped Round Steak accompanied by a mouthwatering Ruby Red Bordelaise Sauce.

Descriptions of this kind give the guests something to chuckle about and help to create a gay mood suitable for dining.

It is true that poetic writing is out of place in many types of copy—especially in "nuts and bolts" copy where specific facts are available. But in describing items where facts are *missing, missing, missing*—and where a certain mood is desirable, poetic copy may be the solution. Poetic style in advertising is like garlic in cooking—a little is okay, once in a while.

HUMOROUS COPY

Readership surveys show that in order to get high readership, you have to GIVE the reader SOMETHING OF VALUE in exchange for the time it takes him to read your copy.

Sometimes a straight sales talk will get high reading. For example, if a man is interested in buying camping equipment, he will read the detailed descriptions of tents and portable stoves in a mail order catalog.

But there are other kinds of sales talks that usually get low reading. For example, a sales talk about the QUALITY of your product. Few people will take time to read paragraphs of copy about "finer, smoother, longer lasting quality, etc." Therefore, if you have a low-interest message to tell, you should give the reader some kind of *inducement* in order to get him to read it. One inducement that increases readership is humor. Give the reader some laughs!

Of course, you can't spend all of your client's money just giving out chuckles and chortles. But if you can skillfully mix laughs with sales talk, you can make both the reader and the client happy. You can make your ad a mutual joyride!

One of the oldest examples of telling a quality story in a light-humorous manner, was the famous series of cartoon ads for Kelly-Springfield Automobile Tires. Here is one of the ads:

(Picture) *A night scene. A car is parked at the curb, with headlights turned on. Two men are chatting and smiling as they enter the car.*

(Copy) *"Well, Bob, it's five minutes past two. What's the story going to be?"*

"Oh, I'll tell her we had a blowout."

"That would never get past MY wife. She knows I use Kelly-Springfield."

A more recent example of humor in copy is the Arrow Shirt series. Ads that talk about the non-shrinking qualities of shirts could be very dull if written in the manufacturer's "claim and boast" style. However, the readership can be stepped up by injecting humor. Here is an example:

(Picture) *Cartoon of a horse sitting down in the street. Milk wagon in background. A man is talking earnestly to the horse.*

(Headline) *My friend, Joe Holmes is now a horse.*

(Copy) *Joe always said when he died he'd like to become a horse.*

One day Joe died.

Early this May I saw a horse that looked like Joe drawing a milk wagon.

I sneaked up to him and whispered, "Is it you, Joe?"

He said, "Yes, and am I happy!" I said "Why?"

He said, "I am now wearing a comfortable collar for the first time in my life. My shirt collars always used to shrink and murder me. In fact, one choked me to death. That is why I died!"

"Goodness, Joe," I exclaimed, "Why didn't you tell me about your shirts sooner? I would have told you about Arrow shirts. They never shrink."

Elsie, the Borden Cow, is the heroine of a series of famous ads that get laughs and readership. Here is one:

(Picture) *Cartoon of smiling doctor examining Elsie, the cow. Elsie is smiling back at the doctor.*

(Headline) *"Oh, Doctor, I bet you tell that to all the girls!"*

(Copy) *"Nothing of the kind, Elsie," the veterinarian answered briskly. "A lot of cows think I'm a fussy old crank. But I promise you I'm going to stay that way—just as long as I'm on this job of keeping you healthy. That's one way we make sure that Borden's Ice Cream is always pure and delicious."*

"Ice Cream? What have you and I got to do with that?" asked the puzzled Elsie, pointing a neatly turned horn at the tempting plateful.

"Nearly everything, my dear," he explained patiently. "If any food—like ice cream—is made from milk or cream, naturally better milk or cream will help make it a better food."

Etc. . . . etc. The conversation continues and the good points about Borden's Evaporated Milk, Borden's Cheese and other Borden products are explained.

How about the advertising for a service such as liability insurance? This can be written in a dull manner that will cause readership survey organizations such as Daniel Starch, Inc. to report: "Our interviewers didn't find anybody who read this copy."

On the other hand, you can write about liability insurance in a light vein, and instead of giving your client high blood pressure, you can give him high "Starch!"

Here is a humorous ad that got high readership for American Mutual:

(Headline) THE CURSE OF TOO MUCH MONEY
A SLIGHTLY TALL TALE
BY MR. FRIENDLY

(Copy) *We saved him so much money*
He couldn't even fold it . . .
He hired 40 trucks
And they couldn't even hold it!
He cried, "Since you cured
Our production ills
Even my dollars have
Little dollar bills! . . .
With all the mink coats
My poor wife has got . . .
She wears 5 at a time
Which is Ritzy, but hot!
If you save me more dough,
I'll burst into tears.
You've saved me so much now
It comes out of my ears!"

(Picture) *Cartoon of insurance man, Mr. Friendly, handing*

money to customer and wife. Customer has dollar bills coming out of his ears and wife is wearing several mink coats at the same time.

Summing up: If you want high readership for your copy, give your prospects *something of value* in exchange for the time it will take them to read it. For example, give them some LAUGHS!

HELP FROM MAIL ORDER COPY

One way to get help, when you are writing an ad for a piece of merchandise, is to look through one of the big mail order catalogs. There you will find copy written by ad men and ad women who have to sell or starve. There are no dealer displays or manufacturers' salesmen to help the mail order sales process. Each ad sells or does not sell, depending on what is printed in the ad. And the sales from the ads are recorded at regular intervals. Result: Good copy!

In the big mail order catalogs you will find ads for almost every conceivable item from A to Z, from accordians to zippers. For example, suppose you have to write an ad about paint—about plain ordinary house paint. What are you going to say about it? Are you going to say that it is easy to apply—that it looks nice after it's on?

If your mind seems to be lacking in ideas, you can turn to the house paint section in a mail order catalog and read the copy. For example, you may find something like this:

The extra thick coat, which this paint is designed to give in one application, enables you to expect 5 or more years of wear from only one coat, on surfaces in good condition. You save time by putting on only 1 coat, handle ladders only once. Extra smooth surface dries without brush marks found in regular paints . . . means more wear . . . no ridges to collect dirt. High hiding . . .

*we guarantee one coat to cover any color—even black. Our
whitest paint ever, 35% of pigment is Titanium Dioxide . . . a
high in the amount of this whitest of all pigments. Starts white,
stays white . . . controlled self-cleaning keeps it clean.*

Here is another item picked at random from a mail order
catalog, namely, electric blankets. You may think, as I did,
that there isn't much you can say about an electric blanket
except that it keeps you warm. Here is a sample paragraph
that shows how a mail order writer was able to think of plenty
of good things to say.

*Safety-approved by Underwriters' Laboratories, Inc. Eleven
separate heats . . . holds exactly the heat you select regardless
of weather changes. Pre-warms your bed. No climbing into cold
sheets. No mountains of blankets. This one blanket is all you
need. Launders easily by hand or washing machine. Costs only
about 2¢ a night for current. Just dial your warmth and then
flick the switch. The gentlest kind of warmth spreads over the
bed. Not the fast, high heat of a heat pad . . . but a more
gradual, soothing warmth that lulls you to restful sleep. Has
Pilot Light, on-off switch, and ample extension cord.*

Here is an interesting game you can play. I suggest you try
it some time. It works as follows:

Step 1: Turn to the index of a big mail order catalog and find
some item which you think would be impossible to write copy
about because you can't think of anything to say about it.

Step 2: Turn to the page indicated and read the copy. Most
of the time you will be amazed at the many things the copy
writer found that he could say about the item.

I do not suggest that you should copy the mail order copy.
But I do suggest that you can use it to start your own ideas
flowing.

Another thing you will find that is used often in mail order copy is what I will call the "cause and effect" sentence. An example occurs in the above ad for electric blankets, namely, "gradual, soothing warmth that lulls you to restful sleep." Some ad writers might have merely said "gradual, soothing warmth." This phrase leaves to your imagination the *result* of that warmth. Other writers might have merely stated the result, namely, "lulls you to restful sleep" without stating the cause of that result. But the *combination* of the two ideas makes a stronger sentence than either idea stated alone.

Here are some typical examples of "cause and effect" sentences. For your convenience I have separated the cause and the effect by means of parentheses. Notice that each claim could have been made separately but that in *combination*, one claim helps to strengthen the other.

Free instruction book . . . (*Written in easy-to-follow language*) . . . (*that won't confuse*).

Horsehide shoes for boys . . . (*Real ground-gripping tread*) . . . (*gives your boy sure-footed traction at all times*).

Paratrooper boots . . . (*Triple-stitched at hard wear points*) . . . (*to last through miles of rough and tumble*).

Note: You don't always have to put the cause first and the effect second. You can reverse the process as in the following: Shirt . . . (*The collar fits just right*) . . . (*because it has the same patented innerlining used in more expensive shirts*).

Another thing to notice about mail order copy is that it contains no fancy language, no tricky style that makes the reader think how smart the copy is. Instead, the copy is written in simple, homely, everyday language designed solely to make the reader think how good the product is.

Words Often Used in Mail Order Catalog Copy

A good exercise for an ad writer is to read mail order catalog ads and write down a list of words frequently used. Then use these words in your own copy.

Here are a few sample words taken from a mail order catalog. They are not all short words, but they are all plain, ordinary everyday words that everybody understands.

quality	fine	deep
give	long	heavy
you	full	top
genuine	great	high
sure	comfortable	natural
strong	wide	real
men	smooth	actual
women	special	better
free	extra	best

Words Often Used in Small Mail Order Ads

The small mail order ads you see in newspapers and magazines are usually excellent examples of how to say a lot in a few words. In these ads you will find frequently repeated the plain, ordinary but effective words that everybody can understand at a glance. Here are examples. Use words like these in your own copy.

home	write	satisfied
many	today	customer
earn	send	guarantee
week	booklet	satisfaction
practical	complete	beautiful
time	sample	need
endorsed	big	keep

thousands	gift	news
because	all	future
save	surprising	personal
easy	discover	income
trial	year	take
plan	reliable	protect
secret	get	quick
original	fast	yours

Special Classes of Words

In mail order advertising you can also find special classes of words and phrases that are useful in describing style, beauty, quality, comfort, strength, etc. Here are examples:

Style

smart	charm at a low price
graceful	tailored beauty
alluring	expertly tailored
elegant	youthfully styled
feminine	fashion tailored

Beauty

lovely	luxurious appearance
gay	looks like linen
flattering	high luster
decorative	permanent luster
becoming	looks expensive
handsome	wrinkle-resistant
glamorous	never seems to wrinkle

Quality

smooth	won't shrink more than 2 per cent
firm	gives radiator-like warmth

durable	strong strands on wearing surface
mothproof	dark color hides soil
rustproof	long staple virgin wool
laundry proof	Du Pont's miracle Orlon
finely woven	for year round wear
double stitched	finest workmanship
triple stitched	rich-textured

Comfort

flexible	easy to wear
easy fitting	smooth fitting
adjustable	built-in comfort
extra roomy	(shoes) room to wiggle toes in
kind to your—	soles bend easily with every step

Strength

sturdy	long-wearing
rugged	heavy-duty
husky	heavyweight
tough	reinforced with—
extra tough	extra material at strain points

Active Sentences

Other good elements you will find in mail order copy, especially in the small, telegraphic-style mail order ads, are short, punchy, active sentences like these:

Today more than ever	Try it for five days
Fortunately for you	Judge for yourself
You can now get	We offer you
Here is a new way	Don't pay a cent unless
This test will show	Free proof you can
Authorities have proved	Here is the plain truth

General Claims versus Specific Claims

Mail order advertisers use specific claims instead of general claims whenever possible. In the two lists below, note that the specific claim in the right-hand column is more convincing and believable than the general claim in the left-hand column. (Read across)

General Claim	Specific Claim
Large	Has 23% more space
Old, established	Our 52nd year
Cooks quickly	Cooks in 5 minutes
Easy to prepare	Just mix, stir and serve
Light weight	Weighs only 1½ lbs.
Illustrated	Contains 38 illustrations
Low cost	Only 10¢ a day

EMOTIONAL COPY

I have left emotional copy until the end of the chapter because I want to leave it strongly fixed in your mind.

Emotional copy, if well expressed, and combined with reason-why copy, is probably the most powerful selling device you can use.

Emotional copy can be spoken or written. Either way, it can make a deep dent in the prospect's mind—not only a deep dent but a lasting dent. Here is a story that illustrates this:

When I was ten years old I remember sitting with my grandmother on the porch of her home in Fostoria, Ohio. An elderly farmer, Jed Williams, dropped in to sit with us and chat awhile. I remember two remarks in the conversation.

"Jed, you have plenty of money. Why don't you retire?" said my grandmother.

"I don't want to die!" exclaimed Jed. He shot out the remark with a burst of emotion. You could tell from the look on his face and the tensing of his body and the pained tone in his voice that the remark came from deep down inside of him. The emotion he showed was stronger than when he talked about the price of wheat, although he had talked emotionally about that, too.

Jed explained that several of his farmer friends had retired and that every one of them had died within a year. Jed named their names and told the dates of their passing.

Now this talk by Jed Williams was in effect a sales talk on the advantage of continuing some sort of activity as long as possible.

His talk has stayed in the back of my head all these years. It is one of those things you remember consciously or unconsciously. But in any case, it eventually becomes part of your *subconscious mind*. It becomes part of that submerged portion of your brain that contains your emotions and affects your most deeply held opinions in later years.

Jed's sales talk consisted of two kinds of copy—emotional copy and reason-why copy, as follows:

Emotional Copy: "I don't want to die!"

Reason-why Copy: Names of farmers who died within a year after they had retired.

In the back of my head and in the back of your head are countless impressions that we have gathered from day to day since infancy. The deepest and longest-lasting of these impressions have been driven into our subconscious mind by the force of emotion.

I remember the time a Columbia professor visited our home. My mother was excited. It was an event. The professor talked of many things which I have forgotten but I do recall his remarks on the value of walking as a physical exercise. He said, "Walking is a gentle exercise that affects your whole body. It gets you out into the fresh air and lifts your spirits. When I take my daily walks, I feel well. When I miss my walks I don't feel well."

Now this is a commonplace remark but he lifted it out of the commonplace by saying it emotionally. You could tell that he really meant it when he said it. To this day I can remember his eager facial expression and his high-pitched tone of voice.

When I was eleven years old my father's medical office, where he examined patients, was located in our apartment at 122nd Street and Broadway in New York. I recall the time I staggered, pale-faced and panting into my father's office and said, "I just raced two fellows around the block! . . . I won the race!"

My father looked shocked. He put his doctor's stethescope against my chest and listened to my pounding heart.

"Don't ever do that again!" he exclaimed in an emotional tone I never forgot.

So I never again raced the boys around the block. And in later years I failed to do well in college athletics. I could not bring myself to give that last ounce of effort which athletes have to give in order to win. When I reached the point of near-exhaustion, I could hear my father saying in an emotional tone: "Don't ever do that again!"

Warning: Emotion is such a deeply felt force that it can work two ways—for or against. Properly used, it can work *for* you. But if wrongly used, it can work *against* you.

For example, when a man says to a woman "I love you," the words can have a powerful effect if they express true emotion. On the other hand, when a young baritone broadcasts a song containing the words "I love you," the effect sometimes falls flat because he is not expressing true emotion.

Some of the songs and sales talks that come to you over the airwaves fail to carry as much conviction as they could carry if the broadcasters believed what they are saying. Some announcers use every trick in the book except truth.

The same applies to some of the politicians. They say in effect to the people, "I love you." But in spite of the words, you get the impression that there is little love in them. Their principal emotion is an intense desire to get elected.

You may say, "But how about the case of a good actress? She can say 'I love you' to a popular movie star and make it sound real. How does she do it?"

The answer is that she is in love with *somebody*, or was in love with somebody at one time or other, and when she says "I love you," she is talking to that person, alive or dead. The audience gets the impression that she is talking to the good-looking chap who happens to be standing opposite her at the moment.

You may say, "Doesn't phony emotion work sometimes? Don't undeserving politicians get elected sometimes?"

Yes, they do, in spite of our democratic processes. Regarding elections, one man quoted Lincoln's remark, "You can't fool all of the people all of the time." This seems like a safeguard but it is not a complete safeguard. In order to get elected, you don't have to fool all of the people all of the time. You only have to fool a little over half of the people part of the time. The same applies in manufacturing. Some temporary successes have been based on fooling part of the people part of the time. But in the long run the best men and the best products win.

A Famous Author's Remarks About Emotional Writing

During my last months at college, I did some job hunting in the spring vacation period. After that, I sat down and wrote accounts of interviews I had had with prospective employers.

I sent these accounts to my father who showed them to his novelist friend Sherwood Anderson. Mr. Anderson was kind enough to write my father a letter containing his reactions. The letter is quoted below. It discusses emotional writing. One thing that adds interest to the letter is the fact that Sherwood Anderson was an advertising copy writer before he became a novelist.

My dear Don:
John has been to see all these men during his vacation, has summed them up pretty well, hasn't been fooled much, and yet one feels that he has felt nothing concerning them.

What makes our young men like that?

A boy like John has taught himself to write. Can he teach himself to feel things so that he will have something real to write about? The whole point of my own writing and the only thing that has made it at all distinctive is that in it I have dared let go of my emotions, take a chance, no matter what the reader might think of me as a man.

I myself began writing because I found that on paper I could do what I could not do often enough in my direct personal relations with people. Fear left me and I stepped at once into a world where all the little secret hungers and emotions we all bury so deeply in life could come out and stretch themselves a little.

You are a physician and I am sure you will understand what I mean when I say that in this respect an art is curative to the practitioner of it. What one does in what might be called the fanciful world of the arts after awhile begins to creep into life itself, into the life of reality.

As I read, I wish that John would sometimes lose a little of his correct young writing manner. The best thing that could happen to him would probably be some gigantic blunder that would put him in bad with everyone, really shake him up.

Regarding Professor Blank's literary advice to John, you must know of course that it is fear of revealing self that has kept Blank from becoming an important artist and without knowing it he does, by suggestion, try to put the same fear into this boy.

And at that, I suppose there is nothing on earth one can do but stand aside and watch. It is an absorbing subject to me because it looks as though I have in my own boys the same problem you have in yours.

Sherwood

Emotion Plus Reason-Why

As far as ad writing is concerned, I think the moral of all this is that if you are writing an ad for a product, you should do two things:

1. Use *reason-why copy* in order to tell the reader *factually* how the product works.

2. Use emotional copy in order to tell the reader how happy he will be when he uses the product.

As a matter of fact, in my ad "They laughed when I sat down at the piano," I included both factual copy and emotional copy. Here are examples:

(Factual copy) . . . *I explained to my friends how I saw an ad for the U.S. School of music—a new method of learning to play which cost only a few cents a day! The ad told how a woman had mastered the piano in her spare time at home—and without a teacher. Best of all, the wonderful new method required no laborious scales—no heartless exercises—no tiresome practicing.*

(Emotional copy) . . . *I played on and as I played I forgot the people around me. I forgot the hour, the place, the breathless listeners. The little world I lived in seemed to fade—seemed to grow dim—unreal. Only the music was real. Only the music and the visions it brought me.*

An advertisement which contains both factual and emotional copy is like a popular song which is written in war time to stir people up. The words contain the factual arguments. The music works on the emotions. The words make people nod their heads in agreement. The music brings them to their feet and starts them marching.

Years ago I wrote in my diary some comments regarding reason-why copy and emotional copy as follows:

Mr. Stuart Chase has just written a book entitled "Your Money's Worth" which has caused quite a stir among advertising people. The theme of the book is that most advertising is a waste—that it adds to the cost of products —that when you buy advertised products you often fail to get your money's worth.

Both Mr. Bruce Barton and Mr. Roy Durstine have written answers to Mr. Chase's attack on advertising. Mr. Durstine's answer consisted mainly of reason-why copy. He dissected Mr. Chase's arguments and showed how Mr. Chase had told only one side of the story. He quoted at least a dozen incidents from Mr. Chase's book and showed that they were wrong and tended to mislead the reader. Mr. Durstine's article was counter-arguments and reason-why copy all the way through.

I was glad to read Mr. Durstine's article because it helped me to disbelieve much of Mr. Chase's attack. And I wanted to disbelieve it. Mr. Durstine gave me arguments which I stored away in my mind for some time I might need them.

Then I read Mr. Barton's reply to Mr. Chase. How differently Mr. Barton approached the problem! He didn't bother to quote Mr. Chase's book or dissect it or give counter-arguments in reply to each of Mr. Chase's arguments. Instead, he took the profession of advertising and told what wonders it is accomplishing in improving living standards—how it is forwarding the progress of the human race—how it is really a noble profession. Barton wrote all this emotionally and he wound up with a fine emotional paragraph in which he said, "If advertising is sometimes long winded, so is the United States Senate. If advertising has flaws, so has marriage."

Mr. Barton moved me, swayed me and convinced me of the good qualities of advertising. Mr. Durstine gave me good reason-why arguments I could use to meet attacks against advertising.

I would therefore say that emotional copy and reason-why copy both have their place in advertising. Emotional copy makes the reader want to buy the product. And reason-why copy gives him reasons he can use to justify himself in buying it.

The other day at lunch, a group of advertising agency men were telling a client about the selling power of emotional copy.

"What is emotional copy?" asked the client.

There was silence. Nobody seemed to have a ready reply. Finally one man gave an answer. Then another gave a different answer. The account executive ordered a round of drinks. This activity of ordering drinks helped to relieve the embarrassment caused by the fact that none of the agency men had a good reply to their client's simple question. Apparently it was easy to talk about emotional copy but it was not easy to define it.

And so, before we close this chapter on copy writing, let's look at a few more examples of emotional copy. Here is a charity appeal which was mimeographed and routed around our office.

December 14

TO EVERYONE IN BBDO

Mary Kenney and Jean Rindlaub and Olive Plunkett and Jo Smith and a lot of people around here thought the editorial from Vogue typed below so tremendous that it would be worth reprinting for everyone in BBDO. We know there are a million demands on your heart this Christmas—but how about 50¢ shoes! Send your 50¢ like an angel to Pearl Popick. She'll see that it goes to the Foster Parents' Plan, Inc.

VOGUE'S EYE VIEW OF 50¢ SHOES

They're entirely of rubber, even their soles. They come in small sizes—children's sizes. They were designed specifically to help Korean children walk through the coming winter (traditional American shoes are not built for the ice-caked slush of roadless Korea). Fifty cents buys a pair. Giving that fifty cents is the exact equivalent of taking a child's foot into your hands and warming it between your palms. But warming a Korean child's cold foot is much more than a matter of providing comfort: it is a specific against amputation—terrifyingly frequent in frost-bitten Korea. That's why Foster Parents' Plan, Incorporated, devised the fifty-cent shoe. It's quite a thought, around Christmas time, to realize that such a small, immediate goodness can reach so far into space—and time. And that's why, in this issue of presents, we place it before all others, as the best buy in the book. Address for contributions: Foster Parents' Plan, Inc., Box 944, New York 8, N.Y.

AUTOMOBILE COPY

How about *product* advertising, let us say automobiles? Cars are usually sold with claims of "more power . . . latest style . . . new gadgets, etc." But cars can also be described emotionally. For example:

(Picture) Old-fashioned auto showroom

(Headline) WHEN HEAVEN WAS AT THE CORNER OF SYCAMORE AND MAIN

(Copy) *Back home, when I was a boy, there was a place at*

*the corner of Sycamore and Main that was as wonderful to me
as anything out of a fairy tale.*

*For on that corner was the Packard showroom. Just about
once a year, father would go there, and he always took me with
him.*

*We never actually bought a Packard, for father's income was
never more than modest. But we got a great kick out of feasting
our eyes on those magnificent cars and imagining what it would
be like to own one.*

*This year, my wife and I decided we needed a new car. As
we passed the Packard showroom I said, "Let's go in, just for
the fun of looking," exactly as my dad used to do . . .*

WARTIME COPY

Most of the time in writing advertisements you have to sell
people on the idea of BUYING something. But in wartime you
are faced with *shortages.* You have to go into reverse and induce people to do without certain goods and services.

Here is a condensed version of an ad selling the idea of reduced train service during World War II. It is one of many examples of emotional copy used in times of emergency.

(Picture) Young soldier in berth on train
> (Headline) THE KID IN UPPER 4

(Copy) *It is 3:42 a.m. on a troop train. Men wrapped in
blankets are breathing heavily. Two in every lower berth. One
in every upper.*

*This is no ordinary trip. It may be their last in the U.S.A.
till the end of the war. Tomorrow they will be on the high seas.*

*One is wide awake .... listening . . . staring into blackness.
It is the kid in Upper 4. Tonight, he knows, he is leaving behind
a lot of little things—and big ones.*

There's a lump in his throat. And maybe—a tear fills his eye.

It doesn't matter, Kid. Nobody will see . . . it's too dark.

Next time you are on the train, remember the kid in Upper 4. If you have to stand enroute—it is so he may have a seat. If there is no berth for you—it is so that he may sleep . . .

MEMORIAL COPY

How do you go about selling granite memorials to the relatives of departed loved ones? This is a difficult subject and must be handled with care.

Do you say "Our granite has been tested and approved?" Do you say "Our memorials are preferred by thousands?" The fact is that the customary sales approaches sound awkward.

The makers of Barre Granite Memorials ran the following copy based on emotion and won an advertising award.

(Picture) Railroad station. Woman waving goodbye to distant train.

(Headline) AUNT MEG . . . WHO NEVER MARRIED

(Copy) *I remember the night Jim Foster went off to the war . . . that last brave flutter of the handkerchief . . . and the sigh of the whistle as the train crossed the bridge over Matthews' Falls.*

Aunt Meg never talked about Jim Foster. She lived with us till we grew up, moving through all the golden memories of childhood . . . the sound of her voice reading in the dim room the time Jane and I had measles . . . her hands arranging roses in a silver bowl on summer mornings . . . the far-away songs she used to sing.

Aunt Meg never married. And the hopes that echoed in her smile departed with the flutter of the handkerchief, the train whistle sliding into silence behind the mountains.

Aunt Meg died ten years ago, gone to her memories, and leaving happy memories behind.

When someone we love has passed away, we face the problem of a suitable memorial . . .

DIAMOND COPY

Emotional copy can also be used in cheerful situations, for example, in selling diamonds.

(Picture) *Bridal couple on vacation*

(Caption) *Honeymoon at Sea Island*

(Copy) *How fair has been each precious moment of their plans come true . . . their silent meeting at the altar steps, their first waltz at the gay reception, and now, these wondrous days together in a world that seems their very own. Each memory in turn is treasured in the lovely, lighted depths of her engagement diamond, to be an endless source of happy inspiration. For such a radiant role, her diamond need not be costly or of many carats, but it must be chosen with care . . .*

HAMILTON WATCH

Here is a Christmas gift ad written by Carl Spier. It has been reprinted for years in Christmas gift issues of publications and has brought many letters of praise. It was reproduced in Perry Schofield's book *100 Top Copy Writers and Their Favorite Ads.* After this book was published, the 100 top copy writers were asked to select which *one* of all the ads in the book they would most like to have written themselves. This ad for Hamilton received the most votes.

Picture: Woman with happy expression is holding wrist watch and letter. Christmas decorations in background.

Copy: At the bottom of the ad is factual copy which describes Hamilton Watches and shows various models. At the top of the ad is the main body of the copy. It is set in the form of a letter from a man to his wife.

To Peggy—for marrying me in the first place . . .
for bringing up our children—while I mostly
sat back and gave advice.
for the 2,008 pairs of socks you've darned.
for finding my umbrella and my rubbers
Heaven knows how often!
for tying innumerable dress ties.
for being the family chauffeur, years on end.
for never getting sore at my always getting
sore at your bridge playing.
for planning a thousand meals a year—
and having them taken for granted
for a constant tenderness I rarely notice
but am sure I couldn't live without
for wanting a good watch ever so long . . .
and letting your slow-moving husband
think he'd hit on it all by himself
for just being you . . . Darling, here's your
Hamilton with all my love!

Jim

13

Ten Ways to Make Ads Believable

1. BE SPECIFIC

HAVE YOU read this ad, 'Retire on $90 a Month,' that has been running in our paper?" asked Les Davis of *The Wall Street Journal*.

"No," I replied. "I didn't believe the headline so I didn't read the copy."

"Read the copy," said Les.

I read the copy and found that it packed more sales punch into small space than any ad I had read in a long time. But more surprising was the fact that in one minute's reading time my disbelief in the headline was shaken. I thought "Maybe it IS possible to retire on $90 a month."

You may not go along with me on this, but I wish you would read the copy and see if it doesn't have a similar effect on you. Try not to be bothered by the many abbreviations. The copy writer used abbreviations in order to crowd his message into small space.

RETIRE ON $90 A MONTH *or less in a resort area, 365 days of sun a year, dry temp. 65°-85°. Or maintain lux. villa, servants, ALL expenses $150-250 a mo. Am.-Eng. colony on lake 60 mi. long. 30 min. to city of ½ million, medical center. Schools, arts, sports. Few hours by air. Train, bus, PAVED roads all the way. Full-time servants, maids, cooks, $6 to $15 a mo., filet mignon*

*35¢ lb., coffee 40¢, gas 12¢ gal. Gin, rum, brandy 63¢-85¢ fifth,
whiskey, $1.50 qt. Houses $10 mo. up. No fog, smog, confusion,
jitters. Serene living among world's most considerate people.
For EXACTLY how Americans are living on $50-$90-$150-
$250 a mo., Airmail, $2.00; 110 Pages current info., prices, roads,
hotels, hunting, fishing and living conditions from Am. viewpoint (Personal check OK) to Peter Arnold, Box 1B, Lake
Chapala, Mexico.*

"Oh, it's in Mexico!" I exclaimed after reading the copy. "I
have never been to Mexico so I'm ready to believe that anything
can happen there. It's a good thing the copy writer put the word
Mexico last instead of first. Otherwise a lot of people might
skip the copy."

The main thing I want to point out is that this copy made
me believe a statement that was previously unbelievable, namely,
"Retire on $90 a month." And the copy altered somewhat my
feeling regarding a trip to Mexico. Previously I had thought "It
is a land of cactus and desert. I'm not interested in going there."
Now I thought, "It might be fun to go there sometime."

How did the copy accomplish this change in attitude?
Answer: *By including a lot of specific facts and figures.*

How about ads that sell a *product*? How do you make product
advertising specific and therefore believable? You can do it by
telling specifications. You can talk about materials and construction and workmanship. For example if your prospective
customer is interested in camping equipment, he will be glad to
read copy such as the following paragraph about Higgins umbrella tents, and it will help to build his confidence.

*Heavy, water-repellent drill, forest green color. Lap felled, double
stitched seams. Tape-reinforced corner seams. Double thick at
eaves. Stitched, rust resistant work rings. Extra reinforcing patch*

*at peak. Detachable, knotted rope stake loops for anchoring
tent. Sewed-in floor—double thick where frame rests. Net rear
window, storm flap. Overlapping net door. All poles, stakes,
ropes are included.*

2. USE TESTIMONIALS

Here are some words that jumped out at me from a newspaper
ad about a new motion picture: Tremendous! Beautiful! Dazzling! Dynamic!

My first reaction was that this was the same old Hollywood
ballyhoo that has been published for years. Sometimes it is true.
Sometimes it isn't. I was reminded of the lament of the copy
writer who was assigned to write an ad for a fifty-cent cigar. He
said, "Everything I can say about a fifty-cent cigar has already
been said about a ten-cent cigar!"

When I looked at the motion picture ad more closely, I found
that something had been added to the claims which increased
believability. Here is how the copy was actually printed:

"Tremendous . . . done in colors of which Rembrandt might
be proud!"—Crowther, *The New York Times*

"Astoundingly beautiful!"—Kate Cameron, *Daily News*

"One of the most dazzling pictures ever made!"—Zinsser,
Herald Tribune

"Never has been played with such electrifying dynamic impact!"—Cook, *World-Telegram & Sun*

The moral of this is that to increase believability you should
include statements from people who are not selfishly interested
in selling the product. These statements can be from famous
people like the Duchess of Windsor or plain testimonials from
plain people.

In using testimonials, it is helpful to sign them with an actual
name and address, if possible. For example:

"I've tried all kinds of scouring pads but these are the best," says Mrs. Emerson P. Holt of 227 Maplewood Drive, Pottstown, Pa.

In case the testimonial giver does not want the actual name and address published, you may be able to use *initials*, as follows:

"I got rid of dandruff with a single application," says K. L. P. of Washington, D. C.

Another method is to sign the testimonial with the individual's vocation, like this:

"Best grape juice I ever tasted," says a housewife.

"School children love it," says a teacher.

3. FEATURE THE NAME OF THE MANUFACTURER

Chapter 8 tells how ads which included in the headlines the names of well-known companies such as Du Pont and General Electric brought more response than ads which omitted these names.

A sales test was made in a store which illustrated the same point. Two identical racks of kitchen utensils made of United States Steel were displayed, side by side.

One display featured the fact that the utensils were made of United States Steel. The other display failed to mention this fact.

Result: The utensils identified as "United States Steel" outsold the non-identified utensils.

After that, the price tags on the non-identified items were reduced so that the prices were slightly lower than the prices of the United States Steel utensils. Result: The United States Steel identified items continued to sell better.

The names of well-known companies can be featured in a number of ways—in headlines, in subheads, in copy, in illustrations, and in logotypes at the bottom of ads.

If your company is not well-known you may still be able to

reap some of the benefits of well-known names by talking about
materials such as—made of United States Steel, made of Du
Pont Orlon, motor made by General Electric.

4. BUILD CONFIDENCE IN THE MANUFACTURER

Suppose your company is not well known but is an old and
established company? What do you do? The answer is that
you should tell the prospect that important fact. Examples:

Blackstone School of Law . . . Founded 1890
Mail order jeweler . . . Diamond specialists since 1882
School of Nursing . . . Our 52nd year
Maker of men's shirts . . . This manufacturer has made
nothing but high-quality shirts for 26 years.

How about a recently introduced product such as a meat
tenderizer? Some readers may say, "If this product is powerful
enough to make a tough steak tender, what will it do to my
stomach?" Here is the first paragraph of an ad that ran in the
Reader's Digest that helps to overcome this fear.

*For centuries, the wholesome fruit of the papaya plant has been
known to make a tough meat tender. Chefs everywhere have
long used papaya extracts to insure tenderness in all cuts and
grades of meat. Now, the full tenderizing qualities of healthful
papaya have been scientifically captured and combined with
other pure foods in Adolph's Meat Tenderizer.*

5. TELL A DRAMATIC TEST OF QUALITY

B. F. Goodrich showed photos of tubeless tires running over
sharp spikes and automatically sealing punctures without losing
air pressure.

The makers of Timex Waterproof Wrist Watches used the
headline "Turtles Test Timex" and showed a photo of turtles
swimming in a glass fish bowl. Each turtle had a wrist watch

strapped around his mid-section. The copy said: "The watches all kept running right on time."

The makers of Fiberglas Screening used the heading "Snaps back without a dent." The ad showed a photo of a youngster using his foot to kick open a screen door.

Sears-Roebuck printed the following story about Biltwel Shoes for children:

Biltwels are given actual wear tests at an orphanage. Active children give them as rugged scuff-scrape wear as any child gives his shoes. That way we find out which materials will give the best service in children's shoes. Take the nylon thread test, for instance. 41 children at the orphanage were each given one shoe sewn with the usual cotton thread. The shoes were checked for wear at regular intervals. The test proved that nylon thread was far superior. That's why we use it in Biltwels.

6. USE REALISM IN COPY AND ART

Use testimonials that sound as if they were written by real people (even if the grammar sounds a bit awkward).

Use photographic illustrations that show the prospect what he actually gets. For example, a restaurant owner gave out discount cards which said, "This card is good for 50¢ towards a $1.89 Steak Dinner." On the reverse side of the card was an actual photo of the steak dinner, showing all the courses in full color.

In showing pictures of people, use models that don't look like models.

If possible, take pictures in actual locations instead of in studios.

Avoid too much retouching of photos. The famous Listerine ads use unretouched photos.

In broadcasting, use announcers that sound natural, not

artificial. Use announcers that sound as if they believe in the products they sell.

7. STATE APPROVAL BY EXPERTS
Here are examples:
Endorsed by dental specialists
Has Good Housekeeping seal of approval
Tested by U.S. Testing Laboratory
Certified by Certified Public Accountants
Won gold medal award
Recommended by 17 washing machine manufacturers
Built of U.S. Government graded materials

A mail order jeweler included this line in his ad. References: "Dun & Bradstreet . . . Jewelers' Board of Trade . . . Or your own bank."

8. GIVE PROOF OF POPULARITY
For example:
"Over eleven hundred sets have been sold"
"Eighteen thousand letters from satisfied customers"
"102,000 policyholders"
"At the best stores everywhere"
"Served by more restaurants"
"Most popular with youngsters"
"More mothers depend on it"
"Carries more passengers"
"Three and a half million packages sold last year"

9. INCLUDE A GUARANTEE
Vic Schwab's famous ad for Dale Carnegie's book included the following paragraph:

It is not necessary to send any money now. You may pay for "How to Win Friends and Influence People" when it is de-

livered—with a definite understanding that its price of only $1.96 will be refunded to you if you wish. If this book does what we claim, it will mean more to you than any book you have ever read. If it doesn't, we do not want you to keep it.

The owner of famous Klein's Department store in New York helped to build his business with the same formula. An enormous billboard on the front of the store which can be read a quarter of a mile away says "MONEY BACK IN 7 DAYS."

Horticultural advertisers include copy like the following:

MONEY BACK GUARANTEE

We guarantee your complete satisfaction—your money back in 10 days or your plants replaced free of charge if notified within 60 days. So for the garden of your dreams, for fabulous flowers that bloom by the thousands, year after year, mail no-risk coupon at once!

On the first page of the Sears, Roebuck catalog, the following panel of copy is prominently featured:

SEARS GUARANTEE

We guarantee that every article in this catalog is honestly described and illustrated.

We guarantee that any article purchased from us will give you the service you have a right to expect.

If for any reason whatever you are not satisfied with any article purchased from us, we want you to return it at our expense.

We will then exchange it for exactly what you want, or will return your money, including any transportation charges you have paid.

10. REPEAT IMPORTANT POINTS

The Social Security Administration in its literature offering information on your Social Security account gives the reader a double warning as follows:

It is not necessary for you to pay anyone to aid you in securing this information. There is no charge for this service.

A mail order copy writer wanted to emphasize that a certain booklet was *free*. And so he mentioned it in different words in different parts of the ad: "This booklet will be sent without charge" . . . "You don't have to pay a penny for this booklet" . . . "Send for this free booklet today."

The Bible uses repetition to drive home important points. Example: "Ask, and it shall be given you; seek, and ye shall find; knock, and it shall be opened unto you."

The value of repetition was summed up by one of Lewis Carroll's fictional characters. This chap was fond of repeating anecdotes. He reassured his listeners with these words: "What I tell you *three times* is true!"

For your convenience, the ten ways to increase believability are listed below:

1. *Be specific.*
2. *Use testimonials.*
3. *Feature manufacturer's name.*
4. *Build confidence in the manufacturer.*
5. *Tell dramatic test of quality.*
6. *Use realism in copy and art.*
7. *State approval by experts.*
8. *Give proof of popularity.*
9. *Include a guarantee.*
10. *Repeat important points.*

14

Six Ways to Prove It's a Bargain

I WONDER IF the price is too high? . . . Maybe I am being
gypped? . . . Maybe I can get a better bargain somewhere
else? . . . Do I need such an expensive model?"

Questions like these often occur in people's minds and stop
them from buying.

To overcome price resistance, *you must prove the value of
your proposition.* You can do this in several ways. In some
cases, you can do it in a few words. In other cases you need to
tell a longer story. Here are examples:

1. TELL HOW THE PRICE HAS BEEN REDUCED

You will recall that Chapter 6 tells the story of how a mail
order book publisher demonstrated the value of a self-improvement book. He began by quoting a high price and then worked
down, step by step, to a low price, as follows:

Step 1. Early in the ad, the copy said that fees ranging as
high as $500 had been gladly paid to the author of the book
for *personal instruction.*

Step 2. Later in the ad, the copy said that many people could
not attend the lectures in person and so the author was prevailed upon to put his methods into book form . . . "Prices up
to $100 were gladly paid for one single book!"

Step 3. Later the copy said:
Until recently these teachings have been available only to the

extremely rich—people who could pay $50 to $100 each for in-struction books. But now, through the efforts of a group of students, these wonderful advantages are within reach of every-one. As a special introductory offer, this important work is now offered to you at the amazingly low price of only $3.

Here is how an advertiser of garden supplies proved the value of his proposition:

Complete Spring Garden Special! All 11 offers in this ad total-ing 431 bulbs—plus an exciting collection of 100 hardy bulbs—a grand total of 531 bulbs—only $10.95. These 531 popular and unusual imported bulbs are actually worth $20.60. Order now—you save $9.65!

Here is how a mail order copy writer handled a price reduc-tion on H. G. Wells' book *Outline of History.*

At One-Third the Original Price! Think of it—a discount of 67% from the price that 50,000 people have already paid!

The greatest users of price reduction copy are the department stores. You will find examples every day in newspaper ads and dozens of examples on Sundays. In fact, if a visitor from the planet Mars should look through the ad pages of one of our Sunday newspapers, he would get the impression that the great-est blunderers in the world are the department store people. Because apparently they are constantly being forced to sell vast quantities of merchandise at prices far less than originally in-tended! However, these advertisers are not blunderers at all. They are simply cashing in on the well-known human desire for a bargain. Here are typical headlines:

SOFAS MADE TO SELL AT $329 . . . $198

CULTURED PEARL NECKLACES, USUALLY $80

... NOW ONLY $39.95

ITALIAN CALFSKIN HANDBAGS $19
... FORMERLY TO $39.95

CHAIRS USUALLY $159 . . . $98.95

BATHING SUITS $8.95 . . . WERE $12.95 TO $19.95

NEW G.E. REFRIGERATOR . . . YESTERDAY $329
. . . NOW ONLY $229

2. DRAMATIZE THE LOW PRICE

In case you cannot feature an actual price reduction, you can
use certain devices to prove that the price is low. For example:

ONLY 10¢ A DAY

AS LITTLE AS $1.50 A WEEK, AFTER
SMALL DOWN PAYMENT

AT THE COST OF ONLY A PACK OF
CIGARETTES A DAY

NO MORE THAN YOU WOULD PAY
FOR A PAIR OF THEATER TICKETS

ONLY 10% ABOVE WHOLESALE PRICES

Bruce Barton, in his most famous ad for the Alexander
Hamilton Institute Course, said, "Is it worth a few pennies a
day to have such an experience?"

A real estate advertiser said, "Charming home . . . 60-minute
drive from New York. Could not be reproduced for double
the price of $38,500."

An ad for a Florida Guide Book said, "Price only $2, only a
fraction of the money you would spend needlessly if you went
to Florida without this information."

A shop selling made-to-order shirts said:

$4 more buys a whole year's supply . . . You wear out four shirts a year on average. Since our shirts, made to measure, cost only $1 more than ready-mades, taking fabric for fabric, you can see that the luxury of a whole year's supply of shirts made to measure, actually costs you only $4 more.

3. TELL HOW OTHERS ARE PAYING MORE

The award-winning ad with the headline "Imagine Harry and Me advertising our Pears in Fortune" contains a list of prices and then says: "At these low prices, these pears cost a mere fraction of what you would pay for them in fine restaurants and hotels."

An ad for Cadillac cars used this same appeal by saying that there are eleven models of other cars that are more expensive than Cadillac.

A car insurance advertiser got good response by using ads with the headline "Car insurance at lower cost if you are a careful driver." This implies that certain people (reckless drivers) have to pay more than you do for car insurance.

4. GIVE THE REASONS FOR THE LOW PRICE

One way to make the bargain appeal effective is to give a *valid reason* for the low price. Here is a story that illustrates this:

A shipping clerk in a mail order concern, made a mistake and packed 200 beauty kits in *plain packages* instead of in the usual *fancy packages*. An ad was run in which the copy admitted this error and said in effect: "A shipping clerk's error is your gain. You may buy our $3 beauty kit for only $2 if you will accept it in a *plain wrapper* instead of in a fancy wrapper."

This ad pulled so well that the shipping clerk was permitted to make the same error over and over, so that the same ad could be repeated over and over!

It is not necessary to go to such extremes in order to find a

SIX WAYS TO PROVE IT'S A BARGAIN 209

reason for low price. For example, here is how Nettleton Shoe Shops did it:

Recently discontinued styles *were $24.95 . . . now $17.88. Year-round styles in* broken sizes *were $22.95 . . . now $13.88.*

Here are other examples taken from newspaper ads:

Five Piece Italian Provincial Bedroom $495 (regularly $1050). Save over $500. The maker went out of business. We purchased all of his remaining stock.

Air conditioners—all brand new, factory-crated. We have no room to store them. In fact, we are overflowing onto the sidewalks. We must sell them fast. So you save plenty.

Before taking inventory, we must greatly reduce our present stock. To do this, prices have been brought down to unprecedented lows.

Greatest sale in our history! Because our warehouses are bulging. Because we have to make room for new Fall stock. Because we snapped up some sensational manufacturers' closeouts.

Mail order necktie salesman, Webb Young, says in his couponed ads:

By selling direct from the weaver to you—I am able to give you these fine ties for only $1.00 each, postpaid.

Here is what Sears-Roebuck said in an ad directed to smokers:

Imported English Briar Pipe . . . $1.98. Before recent devaluation of English money these superb Golden Grain pipes would have cost $3.50.

Included in the introductory pages of the Sears-Roebuck catalog are the following statements giving *reasons* for low prices:

1. Modern equipment eliminates the cost of obsolete methods.
2. Year-round planned buying lowers manufacturing expense.
3. Buying skill furnishes the factory with cloth at low cost.

5. SAY IT'S A BARGAIN

In case you cannot mention actual price reductions, you can simply SAY that your proposition is a bargain.

Here is how William Caxton did this in the year 1479, in the first known advertisement printed in the English language:

If anyone, cleric or layman, wishes to buy some copies of service-books, some of which contain two and others three commemorative services, arranged according to the usage of Salisbury Cathedral, which books set forth the services accurately and are printed in the same type in which this advertisement is set, let him come to the place in the precincts of Westminster Abbey where alms are distributed, which can be recognized by a shield with a red central stripe (from top to bottom), and he shall have these books cheap.

Advertisers today rarely use the word "cheap" because it suggest not only cheap price but cheap quality. However, the ingenious brains of modern copy writers have thought up a variety of ways of saying "low price" without mentioning actual figures. Samples:

Bargain priced
Thrifty prices
The low price will amaze you
At a new low cost
At an unbelievably low price
Specially priced to save you money
Excellent value
Marvelous value
Looks far more than its price

The lowest price we know of

These values are unbeatable

At lowest prices ever

Never before a bargain like this

If you can beat our prices—anywhere—for any reason—we will cheerfully refund your money in cash.

At near give-away prices

Below wholesale cost

We won't even compare them to wholesale because our prices are so far below

Our rates are so low we are not permitted to advertise them.

6. BUILD UP THE VALUE OF YOUR PROPOSITION

The famous Dr. Samuel Johnson, in auctioning off the contents of a brewery in London, said: "We are not here to sell boilers and vats, but the potentiality of growing rich beyond the dreams of avarice!"

An advertiser of diamond rings said: "We guarantee this diamond to appraise for at least 50% more than the purchase price or we will refund double the cost of the appraisal. Choose your own appraiser."

A magazine subscription ad said: "Save ½ . . . 22 months of the *Ladies' Home Journal* for only $3.85. These same 22 exciting issues would cost you twice as much—$7.70 if you bought them at the newsstand."

An advertisement in the housewares section of a mail order catalog said: "One gallon of this floor wax covers the average kitchen floor about 30 times."

A Book Club ad said: "Take any three books (values up to $24.25) for $3.95 (with membership).

An ad selling a trial subscription to *The Wall Street Journal* had the headline, "How $6 started me on the road to $10,000 a year."

In a successful mail order ad for a self-improvement course, the bargain appeal reached an all-time high with the headline: "I gambled 3¢ and won $35,840 in 2 years."

Next time you write an ad, why don't you gamble a few words on the bargain appeal? Perhaps you can win some extra sales! The principal methods are summarized below:

1. *Tell how the price has been reduced.*
2. *Dramatize the low price.*
3. *Tell how others are paying more.*
4. *Give REASONS for the low price.*
5. *SAY it's a bargain.*
6. *Build up the value of your proposition.*

15

Nine Ways to Make It Easy to Buy

A<small>DVERTISERS</small> <small>WHO</small> can trace direct sales results from ads have developed tested methods that stimulate ACTION. It is important to use these methods whenever possible. Your copy may make people desire your product or service, but human inertia—the well-known tendency to "put it off till tomorrow" —may stop you from making *sales*.

Methods that stimulate action can be divided into two classes:

1. Methods that make it EASY TO BUY.
2. Methods that make people BUY NOW.

Let us first discuss the methods that make it *easy to buy*. Here they are:

1. TELL WHERE TO BUY IT

A United States Steel Cyclone Fence ad in a New York newspaper listed four nearby addresses at which Cyclone Fence can be purchased.

A newspaper ad for Rogers Peet stores listed three addresses and told not only the avenue number but *the exact crosstown street,* as follows:

600 Fifth Avenue *at 48th Street*

479 Fifth Avenue *at 41st Street*

258 Broadway *at Warren Street*

Ads for department store items tell the store address and also include the *floor*: "Suits, Third Floor"

An ad for women's blouses by Franklin Simon, New York, told the New York address and also listed ten other cities where Franklin Simon stores are located.

A New York newspaper ad for General Tires listed 79 dealers' addresses in New York, New Jersey and Connecticut. Listing dealers' addresses not only helps your customers but also pleases your dealers.

A magazine ad for Du Pont "Dacron" showed a man's suit and said: "About $85 at these and other fine stores (ad listed names of stores in six cities).

In widely circulating ads where it is not practical to list all the dealers, you can say "See your telephone book" or "Consult Yellow Pages." For example, a magazine ad for Evinrude Motors said "See your Evinrude Dealer. Look for his name under 'Outboard Motors' in your phone book."

2. TELL HOW TO GET THERE

A New York newspaper ad for women's coats contained this line at the bottom of the ad: "120 East Broadway . . . 'D' Train Ind. Subway to E. B'way Station."

A newspaper ad for Goldsmith's Office Supplies contained these instructions:

GOLDSMITH'S—THE ONLY STORE REACHED
BY EVERY SUBWAY LINE

Subway	Station
IRT-Lexington-4th Ave.	Fulton Street
IRT-B'way-7th Ave.	Fulton Street
IND-8th Ave.	Broadway Nassau
IND-6th Ave.	Change at W. 4th St. for 3rd Ave.-"A" train
Culver Line	Fulton Street
BMT	Cortlandt Street

An ad for the White Turkey restaurants listed the New York City branches and then said.

FOR COUNTRY DINING

The White Turkey Inn, Danbury, Conn. on Route 7

The Red Barn, Westport, Conn. Exit 41, Merritt Parkway

The White Turkey, Hartsdale, Routes 100A and 100B

A real estate ad for Merrick Estates contained a drawing of an auto map on which "X" marked the location of the model homes.

A real estate ad for Kendall Park Homes contained this paragraph:

Directions: Lincoln or Holland Tunnel or George Washington Bridge to New Jersey Turnpike to Exit #9 (New Brunswick Exit) into Route 1 and then south 8 miles past New Brunswick Circle. Follow signs to property and model homes on Route 27, Franklin Park, N. J.

3. GIVE BUYING INSTRUCTIONS

In soliciting orders, a department store ad for blankets said: *Beyond motor delivery area, add 55¢ for each blanket.*

A department store ad for draperies contained this paragraph:

HOW TO MEASURE

Use a yardstick or steel tape. Determine length of drapery you wish. For apron length, measure from top of casing to bottom of apron. For floor length, measure from top of casing to floor.

A mail order ad for men's gloves said:

HOW TO MEASURE FOR GLOVES

With fingers touching (bend hand slightly), measure around knuckles of right hand (left hand, if you are left-handed). Do not include thumb. Number of inches is correct size. Allow a little extra room for lined gloves.

A mail order ad for plastic rain capes for children said:
Send cash, check or Money Order, or order C.O.D. and pay mailman cost plus postal charges. Specify size: Small: 2½ to 5½ years; Medium: 6 to 10 years.

4. TELL HOW TO ORDER BY TELEPHONE

Many department store ads list telephone numbers. Some stores give specific instructions. For example, a Gimbels ad said:
Suburbanites, call these numbers and save on tolls: Jerseyites dial your N.Y.C. code, then dial PE 6-5100. Westchester: Yonkers 3-8000, Mount Vernon 4-2920; Long Island: Ivanhoe 9-2500; Connecticut: Greenwich 8-4911.

A Saks ad which appeared on Sunday, said:
Phone order board open Sunday 1 PM to 5 PM . . . Monday beginning 8:30 AM. Call Lackawanna 4-7000 or phone free. . . . in New Jersey (within 20¢ calling area) ask Operator for WX 6767.

An ad for TV sets which appeared in *The Wall Street Journal,* said:
For an immediate Free Trial (without obligation) phone and ask for Operator 21 at any of the following: (Ad listed 22 cities and phone number in each city).

An ad for diamond rings in *The Wall Street Journal* said:
Telephone 24 hours daily. Franklin 2-2928, Chicago

An ad for Statler Hotels said:
For immediate hotel reservation service for all Hilton and Statler

Hotels, call LO 3-6900 (Ad listed 25 cities in which Hilton and Statler Hotels are located)

A manufacturer of typewriters urged buying on the installment plan with payments as low as 10¢ a day. It was found that orders by telephone could be increased by telling the prospect the actual words to say on the phone, like this:
Telephone Riverside 9-9200 and say "Tell me how I can get a typewriter for 10¢ a day."

A loan company also found that results from ads could be increased by telling people just what to say, like this:
Telephone Plaza 1-2400 and ask for Miss Miller. Just say, "Tell me what I have to do to get a loan."

If this business of telling people the actual words to say seems unnecessary, remember the popularity of the ready-made telegrams which are sold by Western Union for birthday greetings, Christmas greetings, etc.

Ad writers who have plenty of experience in putting ideas into words do not always realize that certain people without this experience sometimes have difficulty in putting ideas into words.

5. TELL HOW TO ORDER BY MAIL

A department store ad for women's hats said:
Mail orders filled. Allow 10 days for delivery. Add 45¢ outside delivery area.

A department store ad for women's clothing said:
Mail orders filled on all items on this page. Write Bloomingdale's, Box 1544 for sweaters, Box 1546 for blouses, Box 1495 for dresses.

An ad for a book said:
Order your copy by mail today. Send only $4. Or send no money and publisher ships C.O.D. plus postage.

An ad for the Chambord Restaurant in New York described a meal (of frozen dishes) prepared in their own kitchen, and said:
Now ready to be served at the dinner table in your home . . . Send Check or Money Order (No C.O.D.'s Please) F.O.B. Metropolitan New York.

An ad for theater tickets said:
Mail orders filled in order of receipt. Make check or money order payable to N.Y. City Center and enclose self-addressed stamped envelope. Please list alternate dates.

An ad with the headline 6¼ CARAT EMERALD-CUT DIAMOND said in the copy:
Originally $7,500 . . . Sacrifice $3,800. Will ship to your Bank for inspection. Appraisal permitted before purchase.

Newspaper ads selling subscriptions to *The Wall Street Journal* contain this copy:
It costs $20 a year but you can get a trial subscription for three months for only $6. Just tear out this ad and attach check for $6 and mail. Or tell us to bill you.

6. INCLUDE A COUPON OR ORDER BLANK

Mail order ads for a wide variety of products include coupons or order blanks. In addition, a number of ads which are not strictly mail order ads include coupons or order blanks. This method helps the ad to produce mail order sales in addition to store traffic. For example:

IF YOU CAN'T COME IN, SHOP AT HOME
Mail coupon . . . A Macy's Shop-at-Home representative will come to your home with fabric samples from this great sale.

— — — — — — — — — — — — — — — —

Macy's Box 70, N.Y.C.   *(Dept 265)*
Please send consultant with sample for custom:
☐ *Reupholstery*   ☐ *Slipcovers*   ☐ *Draperies*
Name _____ *Phone* #
Address _____ *Apartment* #
City _____ *Zone* _____ *State* _____

An ad for men's socks by Finchley contained this coupon:

Order by Mail
Send .... *Prs. Hose at $3.50 each. Colours* ....
Name ....
Address ....
☐ *Charge*   ☐ *Remittance herewith*
Add 3% Sales Tax in New York City. Add 25¢ Parcel Post outside Metropolitan United Parcel Zone. No C.O.D.'s under $10.

An ad for the South Brooklyn Savings Bank contained this form:

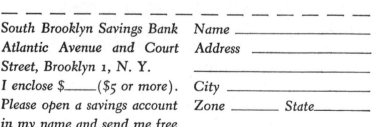

— — — — — — — — — — — — — — — —

South Brooklyn Savings Bank   *Name* _____
Atlantic Avenue and Court   *Address* _____
Street, Brooklyn 1, N. Y.   _____
I enclose $____($5 or more).   *City* _____
Please open a savings account *Zone* _____ *State*_____
in my name and send me free
postage-paid envelopes and
banking-by-mail forms.

                    If you send cash, use registered mail.

An ad for TV sets contained this coupon:

— — — — — — — — — — — — — — —

I would like a Free Trial in my own home. No cost. No obliga-
tion.
Name _____
Address _____
City _____ *Telephone No.* _____
This offer is only available to residents of the 5 boroughs of
New York City, Westchester, Nassau, and Suffolk counties.

7. OFFER AN EASY PAYMENT PLAN

A department store ad for furniture said:
Use Stern's convenient payment account. Pay as little as $6
down, $5 a month.

A Gimbel ad said:
Just 10% down . . . months to pay on our continuous easy pay-
ment plan.

An ad for TV sets said:
As little as $3 a week—3 years to pay.

An ad for Hammond organs contained this offer:
$25 Home Trial Plan. We will place a Hammond Organ in
your home for one, two, or three months for only $25 a month,
including Free Lessons. No other costs. If you decide to buy the
organ during this period, whatever you have paid will be ap-
plied to the purchase price.

An ad for Ranch Homes said:
All models complete, $13,500. Veterans, no down payment. 30
year mortgage, only $91.50 a month.

An ad for new cars quoted a reduced price and said:
While they last! $177 down—3 years to pay—Servicemen financed in 1 hour.

An ad for used cars said:
No money down. 3 years to pay.

A magazine publisher offered Christmas gift subscriptions as follows:
Order your Gift Subscriptions NOW . . . Pay after January 1.

An Airline ad said:
Go Now—Pay Later . . . Signature Travel Plan features no deposit, no down payment, lowest possible financing rate. Get cash for hotels, meals, shopping. Quick action, free of red tape.

An ad for Hathaway's furniture store said:
Which payment method suits your convenience? Take up to 24 months on our Extended Payment Account, with as little as 10% down. Or take 90 days—no service charge—one-quarter down. Or use our 30-Day Charge Account.

8. OFFER A BOOKLET

Many people who read your ad or who hear your commercial are *partly sold* but not completely sold. One way to turn some of these prospects into actual buyers is to offer literature which will do a *complete selling job*. Here are examples:

Free 32-page color-illustrated cook book
Free Book—How to Select Binoculars
Free fashion catalog
Free book—the "Cortina Short-Cut" describes this amazing method and free trial offer

Free photo book of famous strong men

Get free fascinating brochure by Olin Downes, Music in Your Home.

Write today for your valuable free copy of How to Help Your Child Win Success.

Free book, How you can master good English in 15 minutes a day.

I enclose $1. Please send me the "European Holiday" Travel Planning Kit.

3 Free Books . . . 36-page, pocket-size guide to advancement, a gold mine of tips on "How to Succeed." Big catalog outlining *opportunities in your field of interest.*

Send for a copy of our patent booklet entitled "How to Protect Your Invention," *containing information about patent protection and patent procedure. Along with this we will also send you an "Invention Record" form, for your use in writing down and sketching details of your invention.*

Certain booklets should be offered in a plain wrapper. For example:

Maternity styles. Catalog mailed in plain envelope.

Free booklet, What every woman should know *mailed in plain envelope.*

Loans by mail. Application blank sent free in plain envelope.

9. OFFER A SAMPLE

On certain types of products and services, a sample offer may lead to a sale. Here are examples:

Book of Knowledge: Send for "Ride the Magic Carpet," the 24-page, full color booklet taken from the newest revision of The Book of Knowledge. It is FREE and without obligation.

Home gardeners—grow Miracle Tomatoes. Send 10¢ for trial seed packet. Three packets for 25¢.

(Garden Markers) Trial Kit: To acquaint new customers with our markers and labels we prepay three of each style together with a waterproof pencil, all for $1.

Escoffier Sauce: Available at specialty food stores or send $1.10 for your choice of a bottle of Sauce Diable or Sauce Robert to Julius Wile Sons & Co.

Mint-it (Liquid Natural Mint). Send 10¢ for trial size bottle and free folder with tested recipes for Mint-it in many foods and drinks.

Raised Letter Stationery Embosser . . . Write for Free Style Sheets.

Sears, Roebuck Catalog: Free! Yours for the asking. Over 75 actual samples of lovely wall papers.

(Art School) Free Art Talent Test . . . Thousands paid $1 to take this revealing 8-page test. It's yours FREE if you act at once.

(La Salle Institute) Free sample lesson. Also 48-page book, "Accounting, the Profession That Pays" . . . all without cost or obligation.

(Cortina Academy) Free sample record and lesson (check one) ☐ Spanish ☐ French ☐ Russian ☐ German ☐ Italian and complete information about the full Cortina course. Enclosed is 25¢ (stamps or coin) to help cover the cost of special packaging and shipping.

16

Six Ways to Make People Buy Now

Explained below are six methods that help to overcome inertia and induce people to buy immediately.

1. MAKE A SPECIAL OFFER

Here are examples:

(Arthur Murray) Learn to dance . . . Be popular and get more fun out of life . . . Arthur Murray invites you to accept a $1 half hour Trial Lesson.

(Arthur Murray) Got a Lucky Buck? If any of the serial numbers of your dollar bills contain a "5" and an "o" then you've got a "Lucky Buck." And here's what you'll receive for it! A certificate for a $25 Arthur Murray Dance Course at the studio nearest you, plus a wonderful 80-page dance book from which you can learn the Fox Trot, Waltz, Rumba, Samba, Mambo and Jitterbug.

(Lipton Soup Mix) 4-Piece Thermometer and Baster Set only $1 (certified retail value $2.50) and the front from any envelope of Lipton Soup Mix.

(Dale Carnegie Course) You are invited to attend Free Demonstration Meetings in effective speaking and human re-

lations, January 11-12, at 7 PM Sharp, in Dale Carnegie Building, 22 W. 55th St.

Rent a New Car . . . Special offer—if you bring this ad to our rental desk, there will be no mileage charge for the first 10 miles.

Yours Free—as a gift! "Secrets of Married Life" is not for sale, and cannot be bought anywhere at any price. Only a limited number have been printed to be given FREE with this offer: 15 months of True Story for only $2, saving you $1 over regular newsstand price. So don't delay. Act now, save now, while you can . . . and get this wonderful book free.

Electric Shaver . . . Fastest, closest, cleanest shave you'll ever have. Trade-in and 10-day home trial.

G.E. Dealer Trade-in Allowance Coupon. . . . Mail to: Home Laundry Dept.

— — — — — — — — — — — — — — — —

Please ask my nearest G.E. dealer to give me a free trade-in allowance estimate on my old washer. I understand there is no obligation to buy. I now own a . . . . washer . . . . years old.

  Name . . . .
  Address . . . .

Book League of America: Please send me—FREE—the brand-new giant World Globe. Over 3 feet around, shipping weight nearly 7 lbs., 452 sq. inches of map surface, 6410 place names. Enroll me as a member and send me as my Club Selection the best-selling book checked below.

(Murray Hill Restaurant) Starting on February 28th, we are inaugurating an intimate series of table-talks by various per-

sonalities in our lounge. The first speaker, we are delighted to announce, will be the star of a successful Broadway Play. There is no charge, no need to order a thing. Just come (at 3 PM.) listen and be happy under our roof.

Note: In making a special offer, it is sometimes possible to make an offer which will *increase* the amount of the purchase. For example:

☐ *Check here if above order is for two or more items. In this case we send you, without extra charge, a copy of "How to Get Along in this World"—big 160-page volume. This most unusual text is yours to keep even if you return the courses after inspection.*

2. IF THE PRICE IS GOING UP, SAY SO

Examples:

A department store ad said:

Due to rising prices in the raw fur market it is obvious that we may never again be able to offer these low, low prices on fur coats.

An ad for men's wear said:

English overcoats at a special pre-season price . . . $87.50. In season they will be $110.

An ad for a Florida vacation resort said:

"Low summer rates are in effect until December 1st. Now is the time to enjoy a luxury vacation at less than ½ the usual cost."

An ad for new homes said:

Due to rising building costs we cannot guarantee these low prices for more than 30 days.

An ad for the Classics Club said:
Mail this Invitation Form now. Paper, printing, binding costs are rising. This low price—and your Free copies of Plato and Aristotle—cannot be assured unless you respond promptly.

3. IF THE SUPPLY IS LIMITED, SAY SO

Examples:

An ad headed "MAKE MONEY IN SPARE TIME" said:
Only a limited number of Sales Kits available. Write today for yours—sent FREE.

A mail order ad said:
Mail this coupon NOW. This offer subject to cancellation when our present limited stock runs out.

A publisher's ad said:
This may be your last chance to get all 5 for 25¢ (picture of 5 booklets)

Ad for TV-Radio Annual:
Ask your newsdealer to reserve your copy now. Only 50¢. This yearbook sells out as soon as it is placed on sale.

Department store ad:
New Towels—8 for $1.00—Buy Now—Supply limited.

Garden Supply ad:
Hurry! America's finest book of Peonies, Iris and Daylilies will soon be out of print. Send for your copy today.

Plant Nursery ad:
Don't wait . . . Order Now . . . Supplies very limited. We will ship your shrubs at proper planting time.

Phonograph Record Club:

Mail coupon now. We obviously cannot keep "handing out" such magnificent long-playing recordings indefinitely. Production capacity limits the membership rolls. So avoid disappointment. Rush coupon with a dollar today.

4. IF THERE IS A TIME LIMIT, SAY SO

Examples:

There are no "strings" to this offer but it may end soon.

Mail the coupon now before this remarkable offer is withdrawn.

This offer is good for two weeks only.

For this week only—a 25¢ package for only 10¢. Present this coupon to your dealer.

Look lovelier! For a limited time you can get the 40¢ size Noxema for only 29¢ plus tax.

Today is the only time you will see this offer in this newspaper. This is your only chance to order!

Williamsburgh Savings Bank:

Money you deposit here on or before January 14th will earn Dividends from January 1st.

Arthur Murray's Christmas present to you . . . Free—a $25 Gift Course to everyone who enrolls before Christmas . . . Learn the Mambo, or any other dance . . . get a $25 course free to give as a present . . . Come into Arthur Murray's now and receive 2 wonderful dance courses for the price of one. What fun you will have learning and how delighted the lucky person who receives the $25 Gift Course will be!

5. OFFER A REWARD FOR PROMPTNESS

Examples:

Language school ad:

If you act promptly, a valuable French-English Dictionary, containing 45,000 words, will be included without additional cost.

Ad for fish lure:

Free of extra charge! Order Glo-Worm promptly and receive box of 12 sinkers without extra cost.

Ad for children's item:

Autographed picture of Superman in color included Free if you order promptly!

South Brooklyn Savings Bank:

Free Gift for you! Eversharp pen and pencil set—smooth-writing ballpoint pen and matching automatic pencil in attractive gift box—given free to all who open a new savings account with $10 or more during our New Account Festival throughout the month of October.

6. USE ACTION WORDS

In case the specific action devices discussed above, such as "Price going up" or "Supply limited," do not apply to your proposition, you can use *action words*. Here are examples:

Do not delay.

Do not put it off.

Act NOW.

Don't wait another day.

Write now, while this message is before you. It will take but a minute to fill in and mail the convenient coupon.

Write, wire or phone us today. We will get the free sample off to you tonight.

Today—more than ever before—you need this equipment. Mail your trial order NOW.

Tonight serve this ready-mixed chocolate pudding.

(Beauty product) For a girl who expects to be kissed tonight.

Enjoy a luxurious Prell Shampoo tonight.

(Rupture-easer) Delay may be serious. Order today.

Rush name today. Biggest money making weeks just starting.

Don't put off answering this ad even for one day. We need representatives urgently. Send name and addresses on coupon. Hurry! Mail coupon Now!

You need send no money. Right now, without delay, send in your Reservation Certificate. No deposit in advance. First come, first served. Do it now, before you mislay this page!

The average man or woman will put off mailing this coupon till later. Consider yourself above average, with a better-than-average chance of doubling your income, if you mail the coupon now.

Send for "The Secret of Mental Power" now. Do not delay. Do not put it off. Tomorrow you may forget all about it. And the loss will be yours, not ours. For although we have printed an edition of 20,000 copies, we do not expect to have a single one left at the end of 30 days. They are going—and going fast.

Therefore act at once, for as Sophocles so truly said: "Heaven never helps the man who will not ACT."

Summing up: Sometimes good ad writers put so much of their mental power and energy into writing the main body text of an ad that at the end of the ad they are too tired to write more than a weak closing sentence such as "See your dealer."

The closing paragraph of an ad is *important*. To sell or not to sell may depend on how effective you are at the finish. Therefore, the next time you write an ad, try to include one or more of the following action-getting devices that have been described in Chapter 15 and in Chapter 16.

1. *Tell where to buy it.*
2. *Tell how to get there.*
3. *Give buying instructions.*
4. *Tell how to order by telephone.*
5. *Tell how to order by mail.*
6. *Include a coupon or order blank.*
7. *Offer easy payment plan.*
8. *Offer a booklet.*
9. *Offer a sample.*
10. *Make a special offer.*
11. *If the price is going up, say so.*
12. *If the supply is limited, say so.*
13. *If there is a time limit, say so.*
14. *Offer a reward for promptness.*
15. *Use action words.*

17

A Check List for Making Ads Pay

"Go to the proof files and get me a bunch of proofs of mail order ads. Bring them to my desk and I'll tell you which were successful in making sales and which were failures. I want you to study the ads. Try to figure out what the successful ads have got that the failures haven't got. Then when you write your own ads, try to put into them the things that will make them successful."

As told in Chapter I, that was what Copy Chief Ev Grady said to me on the first day of my first job as an ad writer.

After 31 years in the advertising business, I can give you no better advice. Study the failures. Study the successes. Both can teach you something. Not only in advertising but in life itself. Try to figure out what qualities the successes have that the failures do not have. Then put into your own work the qualities that will make your work successful.

Sometimes I have a feeling that it would be fun to turn the clock back 31 years—and wake up some fine morning and find that I am back in Grady's office, standing beside Grady's desk. I wouldn't mind starting all over again.

In fact, wouldn't it be wonderful to start over again—knowing what I know now: I would pay more strict attention to what Grady said. I would try harder to learn from each experience. I might do better if I could have a second chance.

But that is impossible. That is what everybody wants and

nobody can have—youth and experience at the same time. Life does not offer that combination. You begin with youth. You end with experience. Both are wonderful!

"Build thee more stately mansions, oh my soul!—as the swift seasons roll," said the poet Oliver Wendell Holmes. If I ever succeed in getting to Heaven, I hope I'll be sent to Ev Grady's mansion for instruction and guidance. And if I ever win the right to wear a pair of wings, I believe that Grady will say, "John, I want you to go to the wing files and get me a bunch of wings. Bring them to my desk and I'll tell you which can fly and which can't!"

I'd like to have a chance to tell Grady that as far as ad writing is concerned, I have been trying to follow his advice. For 31 years I have studied the ads that failed and the ads that succeeded. I have put into this book the results of that study.

It all boils down to this: There are certain advertisers who can measure the sales results from their advertising. There are others who can't.

The advertisers who can measure sales results have tried many kinds of ads and many selling devices over a period of years. Certain methods and techniques and principles have been discovered that *get results*. These methods and techniques have been repeated again and again in the successful ads. These are the things that you should take to heart. These qualities that are repeated and repeated in the successful, traceable ads are the qualities which YOU should put into YOUR ads in order to make YOUR ads successful.

If you are working on traceable advertising, your way is fairly clear. *Take the best methods that past experience has to offer and use these methods as your own.*

Also, you should, from time to time, experiment with new methods. As BBDO's Board Chairman, Charlie Brower said in an article in *Reader's Digest*, "Discontent and curiosity are two keys to success." In ad writing this means discontent with the old and curiosity to try something new. Use the trial-and-error technique. Test the old against the new. Let the best methods win. *Learn from the failures. Repeat the successes.*

If you are working on advertising where results cannot be traced, you should learn all you can from traceable advertising and transfer that knowledge to the work you do on other types of advertising. Your prospect's human nature does not change when he shifts his attention from a tested mail order ad to an untested institutional ad. If you find that simple language is more effective than fancy language in a mail order ad, you should not suddenly shift to fancy language when you are writing an institutional ad.

Below is an advertising check list of seven tested methods that help to make ads sell. These are the methods that have been repeated and repeated in successful ads. You can't use all of these methods in every ad you write, but you should use all you can. After you have written an ad, you should glance at this check list and make sure you have not inadvertently omitted any of the good time-tested techniques that make ads pay.

Advertising Check List

1. *Get attention.* This is usually done by stating in a few words a *believable promise to the right audience.* Or by showing *a picture of the reward,* which your product offers people.

2. *Hold attention.* This is done with subheads or with sub-illustrations or with a first paragraph which contains one of the attention-holding devices described in Chapter 11.

3. *Create desire.* This is done by *piling up benefits* in the copy you write, as described in Chapter 12.

4. *Make it believable.* This is done by including *specific figures, testimonials, guarantees,* etc., as described in Chapter 13.

5. *Prove it's a bargain.* This is done by talking about *price reductions* and *by building up the value of your proposition* as explained in Chapter 14.

6. *Make it easy to buy.* This is done by telling *where to buy and how to order,* and by other methods discussed in Chapter 15.

7. *Give a reason to buy now.* This is done by including *special offers and rewards for promptness* and other action-getting devices as explained in Chapter 16.

As previously mentioned, you can't include all seven of these methods in every ad or in every broadcast commercial, but you should include all you can.

Some ads do include all seven methods and as an example of this I invite your attention to Walter Weintz' famous ad for The *Reader's Digest* Condensed Book Club. In order to show you exactly how the advertising check list can be applied to checking a specific ad, let us apply it to this book club ad, step by step, as follows:

Step 1—Get attention

(Headline) *READER'S DIGEST* INVITES YOU TO ACCEPT THIS 576-PAGE BOOK FOR 10¢

(Picture) Photograph of book

(Analysis) The photograph of the book attracts the *right audience,* namely a book-loving audience. The headline contains a *promise* which appeals to a book-loving audience. The *specific figures* and the name *Reader's Digest* make the promise *believable.*

Step 2—Hold attention

(Subhead) Yours to Keep . . . No More to Pay!

(Sub-illustrations) Small pictures of five best-selling current books that are condensed in the big single volume which you get for 10¢.

(First paragraph) *This exciting volume regularly sells for $2.32. But we offer it to you—to keep—for only 10¢ to introduce you to* Reader's Digest *Condensed Books.*

(Analysis) The subhead and sub-illustrations *hold* the reader's attention. The first paragraph *holds the reader* by using method number one in Chapter 10, namely, "continue the thought in the headline."

Step 3—Create desire

(Subhead) WHAT YOU GET FOR 10¢

(Copy) The copy lists the titles of the five condensed books and describes the contents of each book and tells the names of the famous authors who wrote the books. The copy also says, "Illustrated in color, beautifully printed and bound."

(Analysis) The copy creates desire by *piling up benefits.*

Step 4—Make it believable

(Subhead) WHAT SOME FAMOUS READERS SAY

(Copy) The copy contains testimonials praising the book club. These are signed by J. Edgar Hoover, Olivia de Havilland and Quentin Reynolds.

(Analysis) These testimonials add believability to the ad which has already been made substantially believable by such elements as specific figures and the well-known name *Reader's Digest.*

Step 5—Prove it's a bargain

(Copy) The Publishers' prices of the five books which are condensed in the single volume are listed after the title of each book, as follows: $3.75 . . . $3.95 . . . $4.50 . . . $4.00 . . . $3.50 . . . Total Original Prices . . . $19.70.

(Analysis) The reader has been told in the headline that **he** can have the volume for only 10¢. In the copy he is told that as a book club member he can have succeeding volumes for only $2.32 plus 12¢ postage. In either case, whether he buys only the first volume for 10¢ or succeeding volumes for $2.32 plus postage, he is obviously getting a bargain.

Step 6—Make it easy to act

The ad makes it easy to act because in the lower right-hand corner of the ad is printed *a convenient order blank*.

Step 7—Give a reason to act now

This is done by including in the copy a time limit as follows: "Because our supply of introductory books is limited, we cannot extend this offer beyond October 3. So please hurry."

IN CONCLUSION

"It is better to light one candle than to curse the darkness"

I quoted the above line from the Bible because it seems to apply to *advertising*. Advertising, like news, is a form of *light*. Said Bruce Barton, "As a profession advertising is young; as a force it is as old as the world. The first four words uttered, 'Let there be light,' constitute its character. All nature is vibrant with its impulse."

This book has discussed advertising from only one point of view, namely, how to make ads pay. In this final chapter, I would like to answer two questions that are often asked, as follows:

1. Is advertising a good business to be in?

2. Does advertising make a worthwhile contribution to our way of living?

I would like to answer these questions by quoting testimonials from people who are not selfishly interested in selling advertising.

I read but one newspaper and that more for its advertisements than its news.—Thomas Jefferson

The pre-eminence of America in industry, which has constantly brought about a reduction in costs, has come very largely through mass production. Mass production is only possible where there is demand. Mass demand has been created almost entirely through the development of advertising.—Calvin Coolidge

If I were starting life over again, I am inclined to think that I would go into the advertising business in preference to almost any other. This is because advertising has come to cover the whole range of human needs and also because it combines real imagination with a deep study of human psychology. Because it brings to the greatest number of people actual knowledge concerning useful things, it is essentially a form of education . . . It has risen with ever-growing rapidity to the dignity of an art. It is constantly paving new paths . . . The general raising of the standards of modern civilization among all groups of people during the past half century would have been impossible without the spreading of the knowledge of higher standards by means of advertising.—Franklin D. Roosevelt

Advertising nourishes the consuming power of men. It creates wants for a better standard of living. It sets up before a man the goal of a better home, better clothing, better food for himself and his family. It spurs individual exertion and greater production.—Winston Churchill

Given a good product, the American advertising industry does an efficient, imaginative and essential job of information and promotion and makes an important contribution. —Dwight D. Eisenhower

Bill Orchard's Ad Writing
Course at Columbia

I would like to end this book with a short autobiographical piece I wrote for *Advertising Agency* magazine. Here it is:

I couldn't get a job as an advertising copy writer, so I took a course in copy writing.

I quit my job at the Certain-teed Company on June 1, 1925, and spent the month of June knocking around New York via the shoe leather route. I knocked on many agency doors. The agency men said: "No . . . Not now . . . Get some selling experience . . . We are filled up . . . Come back later."

So, during the summer of 1925 I took (the late) Bill Orchard's course in ad writing at Columbia.

I liked Bill Orchard right away. He worked for the George Batten Advertising Agency as copy editor. He brought into the classroom the spirit, the jargon, the atmosphere, and the day to day problems of an advertising agency. He acted as copy chief and the 25 men and women students were his copy department.

Bill gave us ad writing assignments. Then he gave us oral and written criticisms on our copy. He told us which ads he would run and which had to be re-written. He read some of our ads aloud in class.

I remember the day we were asked to read our own ads aloud to the rest of the class. I hated this. And it just happened that the assignment for that day had been to write an emotional piece of copy.

My copy seemed so emotional to me as I read it aloud that I

became choked with emotion and could scarcely continue reading. I felt completely ridiculous. In a shaking voice I finally gasped out the last sentence. When I had finished, I heard one of the women students breathe a sigh of relief as if to say, "Thank heaven that's over!"

Bill was especially good at answering questions. Each question from a student brought from Bill some anecdote or some case history from his rich store of experience.

Bill Orchard's course sold me on the idea that taking courses is practical. The ads I wrote in Bill's course enabled me to get a job. My ads were not outstanding. The highest mark I got was an A minus. Most of my marks were B's. But the ads gave me samples to show. And I found that copy chiefs were interested in the samples and in Bill Orchard's typed criticisms attached to the ads.

Now here is a coincidence. A few weeks ago, Bill Orchard told me he was going to take a vacation in Florida. He said, "Will you teach my ad class at Columbia while I'm away?" I said yes.

As I write this I am in the midst of my first classroom teaching experience. I've already given three lectures and I have to give some more. Bill gave me the key to the office, a list of the students, a list of assignments and the class textbook. So I am carrying on until Bill returns.

I found that going back to Columbia was something like returning to church after a long absence. Man's residence on this planet is temporary but the church goes on forever. The same applies to a university. The students come and go but the university is permanent.

I took a course in 1925. I got a job. I went downtown for a while. It seemed just a short while. But in some unaccountable way, the years slipped by and I am back uptown again, on my way to an evening class.

I get off at 116th Street. I can see the Barnard section of Columbia. My mother graduated from Barnard in 1904. I was born while she was a student there. My father was a medical student at Bellevue. An amusing thought occurs to me: "Gosh, I must have taken my first trips to Columbia without knowing it!" Mother used to say, "I got my 'MA' before I got my BA."

I pass the Journalism Building where I studied short story writing and novel writing. Once I thought I could write a novel. Well, never mind. Novel writers starve in garrets. But you can make a living writing ads.

Across South Field I can see Livingston Hall, the dormitory where I lived in 1918. I was in the Columbia Class of 1922. We attended lectures in the morning and drilled in the afternoon— "Squads right! Squads left!"

Some of the boys wore Navy uniforms and some wore Army uniforms. The country was at war. Some went across. Some didn't. Some came back. Some didn't. This was supposed to be the final war—to end war. In December came the government order to take off our uniforms and put on civilian clothes.

As I turn left and go up the stone steps into the School of Business Building, I pass the bench where, as a youngster, I used to sit with mother in the summertime. It is the same bench. It is made of stone. People come and people go but stone benches last forever. She had a book and I had a ball. There was a grass plot where kids could play. The grass is brown now. It is winter. But it will be green again.

Inside the School of Business everything looks the same except the woodwork, which is darker. This is the building where I took Bill Orchard's course in 1925, and Shaw-Thompson's course. The building was new then.

I can see men and women students carrying books. They look about the same—young, eager, hopeful. I can see budding romances in the way some of the boys and girls look at each other. I recall a line of poetry about springtime: "Life again, leaf again, love again!"

Downtown people look worried. As if the world might end. But up here the young folks look cheerful. They know the world is not going to end. It is just beginning!

The notices on the bulletin board and the pile of blue catalogs on the table look the same. The elevator is just as slow as in 1925. Yes sir, everything is the same, and if I can avoid seeing my reflection in the washroom mirror, I can almost imagine that I am the same too.

Downtown things are hectic. Accounts are won. Accounts are lost. New companies are born. Old companies die. Men have worried expressions that three martinis can't wipe off.

But up at the university, things are calm, peaceful, cheerful. Universities don't die. They don't even fade. Two things stand firm—churches and universities. Like rocks in a rushing river. Here's advice. Drop in at one or the other sometime. Light a candle. Say a prayer. Attend a university lecture. Or give a lecture yourself! You will come away feeling refreshed.

Index

A CATALOGUE OF SELECTED DOVER BOOKS
IN ALL FIELDS OF INTEREST

A CATALOGUE OF SELECTED DOVER BOOKS
IN ALL FIELDS OF INTEREST

THE DEVIL'S DICTIONARY, Ambrose Bierce. Barbed, bitter, brilliant witticisms in the form of a dictionary. Best, most ferocious satire America has produced. 145pp. 20487-1 Pa. $1.75

ABSOLUTELY MAD INVENTIONS, A.E. Brown, H.A. Jeffcott. Hilarious, useless, or merely absurd inventions all granted patents by the U.S. Patent Office. Edible tie pin, mechanical hat tipper, etc. 57 illustrations. 125pp. 22596-8 Pa. $1.50

AMERICAN WILD FLOWERS COLORING BOOK, Paul Kennedy. Planned coverage of 48 most important wildflowers, from Rickett's collection; instructive as well as entertaining. Color versions on covers. 48pp. 8¼ x 11. 20095-7 Pa. $1.50

BIRDS OF AMERICA COLORING BOOK, John James Audubon. Rendered for coloring by Paul Kennedy. 46 of Audubon's noted illustrations: red-winged blackbird, cardinal, purple finch, towhee, etc. Original plates reproduced in full color on the covers. 48pp. 8¼ x 11. 23049-X Pa. $1.50

NORTH AMERICAN INDIAN DESIGN COLORING BOOK, Paul Kennedy. The finest examples from Indian masks, beadwork, pottery, etc. — selected and redrawn for coloring (with identifications) by well-known illustrator Paul Kennedy. 48pp. 8¼ x 11. 21125-8 Pa. $1.50

UNIFORMS OF THE AMERICAN REVOLUTION COLORING BOOK, Peter Copeland. 31 lively drawings reproduce whole panorama of military attire; each uniform complete instructions for accurate coloring. (Not in the Pictorial Archives Series). 64pp. 8¼ x 11. 21850-3 Pa. $1.50

THE WONDERFUL WIZARD OF OZ COLORING BOOK, L. Frank Baum. Color the Yellow Brick Road and much more in 61 drawings adapted from W.W. Denslow's originals, accompanied by abridged version of text. Dorothy, Toto, Oz and the Emerald City. 61 illustrations. 64pp. 8¼ x 11. 20452-9 Pa. $1.50

CUT AND COLOR PAPER MASKS, Michael Grater. Clowns, animals, funny faces . . . simply color them in, cut them out, and put them together, and you have 9 paper masks to play with and enjoy. Complete instructions. Assembled masks shown in full color on the covers. 32pp. 8¼ x 11. 23171-2 Pa. $1.50

STAINED GLASS CHRISTMAS ORNAMENT COLORING BOOK, Carol Belanger Grafton. Brighten your Christmas season with over 100 Christmas ornaments done in a stained glass effect on translucent paper. Color them in and then hang at windows, from lights, anywhere. 32pp. 8¼ x 11. 20707-2 Pa. $1.75

CREATIVE LITHOGRAPHY AND HOW TO DO IT, Grant Arnold. Lithography as art form: working directly on stone, transfer of drawings, lithotint, mezzotint, color printing; also metal plates. Detailed, thorough. 27 illustrations. 214pp.
21208-4 Pa. $3.00

DESIGN MOTIFS OF ANCIENT MEXICO, Jorge Enciso. Vigorous, powerful ceramic stamp impressions — Maya, Aztec, Toltec, Olmec. Serpents, gods, priests, dancers, etc. 153pp. 6⅛ x 9¼. 20084-1 Pa. $2.50

AMERICAN INDIAN DESIGN AND DECORATION, Leroy Appleton. Full text, plus more than 700 precise drawings of Inca, Maya, Aztec, Pueblo, Plains, NW Coast basketry, sculpture, painting, pottery, sand paintings, metal, etc. 4 plates in color. 279pp. 8⅜ x 11¼. 22704-9 Pa. $4.50

CHINESE LATTICE DESIGNS, Daniel S. Dye. Incredibly beautiful geometric designs: circles, voluted, simple dissections, etc. Inexhaustible source of ideas, motifs. 1239 illustrations. 469pp. 6⅛ x 9¼. 23096-1 Pa. $5.00

JAPANESE DESIGN MOTIFS, Matsuya Co. Mon, or heraldic designs. Over 4000 typical, beautiful designs: birds, animals, flowers, swords, fans, geometric; all beautifully stylized. 213pp. 11⅜ x 8¼. 22874-6 Pa. $5.00

PERSPECTIVE, Jan Vredeman de Vries. 73 perspective plates from 1604 edition; buildings, townscapes, stairways, fantastic scenes. Remarkable for beauty, surrealistic atmosphere; real eye-catchers. Introduction by Adolf Placzek. 74pp. 11⅜ x 8¼. 20186-4 Pa. $2.75

EARLY AMERICAN DESIGN MOTIFS, Suzanne E. Chapman. 497 motifs, designs, from painting on wood, ceramics, appliqué, glassware, samplers, metal work, etc. Florals, landscapes, birds and animals, geometrics, letters, etc. Inexhaustible. Enlarged edition. 138pp. 8⅜ x 11¼. 22985-8 Pa. $3.50
23084-8 Clothbd. $7.95

VICTORIAN STENCILS FOR DESIGN AND DECORATION, edited by E.V. Gillon, Jr. 113 wonderful ornate Victorian pieces from German sources; florals, geometrics; borders, corner pieces; bird motifs, etc. 64pp. 9⅜ x 12¼. 21995-X Pa. $2.75

ART NOUVEAU: AN ANTHOLOGY OF DESIGN AND ILLUSTRATION FROM THE STUDIO, edited by E.V. Gillon, Jr. Graphic arts: book jackets, posters, engravings, illustrations, decorations; Crane, Beardsley, Bradley and many others. Inexhaustible. 92pp. 8⅛ x 11. 22388-4 Pa. $2.50

ORIGINAL ART DECO DESIGNS, William Rowe. First-rate, highly imaginative modern Art Deco frames, borders, compositions, alphabets, florals, insectals, Wurlitzer-types, etc. Much finest modern Art Deco. 80 plates, 8 in color. 8⅜ x 11¼. 22567-4 Pa. $3.50

HANDBOOK OF DESIGNS AND DEVICES, Clarence P. Hornung. Over 1800 basic geometric designs based on circle, triangle, square, scroll, cross, etc. Largest such collection in existence. 261pp. 20125-2 Pa. $2.75

VICTORIAN HOUSES: A TREASURY OF LESSER-KNOWN EXAMPLES, Edmund Gillon and Clay Lancaster. 116 photographs, excellent commentary illustrate distinct characteristics, many borrowings of local Victorian architecture. Octagonal houses, Americanized chalets, grand country estates, small cottages, etc. Rich heritage often overlooked. 116 plates. 11⅜ x 10. 22966-1 Pa. $4.00

STICKS AND STONES, Lewis Mumford. Great classic of American cultural history; architecture from medieval-inspired earliest forms to 20th century; evolution of structure and style, influence of environment. 21 illustrations. 113pp. 20202-X Pa. $2.50

ON THE LAWS OF JAPANESE PAINTING, Henry P. Bowie. Best substitute for training with genius Oriental master, based on years of study in Kano school. Philosophy, brushes, inks, style, etc. 66 illustrations. 117pp. 6⅛ x 9¼. 20030-2 Pa. $4.50

A HANDBOOK OF ANATOMY FOR ART STUDENTS, Arthur Thomson. Virtually exhaustive. Skeletal structure, muscles, heads, special features. Full text, anatomical figures, undraped photos. Male and female. 337 illustrations. 459pp. 21163-0 Pa. $5.00

AN ATLAS OF ANATOMY FOR ARTISTS, Fritz Schider. Finest text, working book. Full text, plus anatomical illustrations; plates by great artists showing anatomy. 593 illustrations. 192pp. 7⅞ x 10¾. 20241-0 Clothbd. $6.95

THE HUMAN FIGURE IN MOTION, Eadweard Muybridge. More than 4500 stopped-action photos, in action series, showing undraped men, women, children jumping, lying down, throwing, sitting, wrestling, carrying, etc. "Unparalleled dictionary for artists," American Artist. Taken by great 19th century photographer. 390pp. 7⅞ x 10⅝. 20204-6 Clothbd. $12.50

AN ATLAS OF ANIMAL ANATOMY FOR ARTISTS, W. Ellenberger et al. Horses, dogs, cats, lions, cattle, deer, etc. Muscles, skeleton, surface features. The basic work. Enlarged edition. 288 illustrations. 151pp. 9⅜ x 12¼. 20082-5 Pa. $4.50

LETTER FORMS: 110 COMPLETE ALPHABETS, Frederick Lambert. 110 sets of capital letters; 16 lower case alphabets; 70 sets of numbers and other symbols. Edited and expanded by Theodore Menten. 110pp. 8⅛ x 11. 22872-X Pa. $3.00

THE METHODS OF CONSTRUCTION OF CELTIC ART, George Bain. Simple geometric techniques for making wonderful Celtic interlacements, spirals, Kells-type initials, animals, humans, etc. Unique for artists, craftsmen. Over 500 illustrations. 160pp. 9 x 12. USO 22923-8 Pa. $4.00

SCULPTURE, PRINCIPLES AND PRACTICE, Louis Slobodkin. Step by step approach to clay, plaster, metals, stone; classical and modern. 253 drawings, photos. 255pp. 8⅛ x 11. 22960-2 Pa. $5.00

THE ART OF ETCHING, E.S. Lumsden. Clear, detailed instructions for etching, drypoint, softground, aquatint; from 1st sketch to print. Very detailed, thorough. 200 illustrations. 376pp. 20049-3 Pa. $3.75

CONSTRUCTION OF AMERICAN FURNITURE TREASURES, Lester Margon. 344 detail drawings, complete text on constructing exact reproductions of 38 early American masterpieces: Hepplewhite sideboard, Duncan Phyfe drop-leaf table, mantel clock, gate-leg dining table, Pa. German cupboard, more. 38 plates. 54 photographs. 168pp. 8⅜ x 11¼. 23056-2 Pa. $4.00

JEWELRY MAKING AND DESIGN, Augustus F. Rose, Antonio Cirino. Professional secrets revealed in thorough, practical guide: tools, materials, processes; rings, brooches, chains, cast pieces, enamelling, setting stones, etc. Do not confuse with skimpy introductions: beginner can use, professional can learn from it. Over 200 illustrations. 306pp. 21750-7 Pa. $3.00

METALWORK AND ENAMELLING, Herbert Maryon. Generally conceeded best all-around book. Countless trade secrets: materials, tools, soldering, filigree, setting, inlay, niello, repoussé, casting, polishing, etc. For beginner or expert. Author was foremost British expert. 330 illustrations. 335pp. 22702-2 Pa. $3.50

WEAVING WITH FOOT-POWER LOOMS, Edward F. Worst. Setting up a loom, beginning to weave, constructing equipment, using dyes, more, plus over 285 drafts of traditional patterns including Colonial and Swedish weaves. More than 200 other figures. For beginning and advanced. 275pp. 8¾ x 6⅜. 23064-3 Pa. $4.50

WEAVING A NAVAJO BLANKET, Gladys A. Reichard. Foremost anthropologist studied under Navajo women, reveals every step in process from wool, dyeing, spinning, setting up loom, designing, weaving. Much history, symbolism. With this book you could make one yourself. 97 illustrations. 222pp. 22992-0 Pa. $3.00

NATURAL DYES AND HOME DYEING, Rita J. Adrosko. Use natural ingredients: bark, flowers, leaves, lichens, insects etc. Over 135 specific recipes from historical sources for cotton, wool, other fabrics. Genuine premodern handicrafts. 12 illustrations. 160pp. 22688-3 Pa. $2.00

THE HAND DECORATION OF FABRICS, Francis J. Kafka. Outstanding, profusely illustrated guide to stenciling, batik, block printing, tie dyeing, freehand painting, silk screen printing, and novelty decoration. 356 illustrations. 198pp. 6 x 9. 21401-X Pa. $3.00

THOMAS NAST: CARTOONS AND ILLUSTRATIONS, with text by Thomas Nast St. Hill. Father of American political cartooning. Cartoons that destroyed Tweed Ring; inflation, free love, church and state; original Republican elephant and Democratic donkey; Santa Claus; more. 117 illustrations. 146pp. 9 x 12.
22983-1 Pa. $4.00
23067-8 Clothbd. $8.50

FREDERIC REMINGTON: 173 DRAWINGS AND ILLUSTRATIONS. Most famous of the Western artists, most responsible for our myths about the American West in its untamed days. Complete reprinting of *Drawings of Frederic Remington* (1897), plus other selections. 4 additional drawings in color on covers. 140pp. 9 x 12.
20714-5 Pa. $3.95

EARLY NEW ENGLAND GRAVESTONE RUBBINGS, Edmund V. Gillon, Jr. 43 photographs, 226 rubbings show heavily symbolic, macabre, sometimes humorous primitive American art. Up to early 19th century. 207pp. 8³/8 x 11¼.
21380-3 Pa. $4.00

L.J.M. DAGUERRE: THE HISTORY OF THE DIORAMA AND THE DAGUERREOTYPE, Helmut and Alison Gernsheim. Definitive account. Early history, life and work of Daguerre; discovery of daguerreotype process; diffusion abroad; other early photography. 124 illustrations. 226pp. 6¹/6 x 9¼. 22290-X Pa. $4.00

PHOTOGRAPHY AND THE AMERICAN SCENE, Robert Taft. The basic book on American photography as art, recording form, 1839-1889. Development, influence on society, great photographers, types (portraits, war, frontier, etc.), whatever else needed. Inexhaustible. Illustrated with 322 early photos, daguerreotypes, tintypes, stereo slides, etc. 546pp. 6¹/8 x 9¼. 21201-7 Pa. $5.95

PHOTOGRAPHIC SKETCHBOOK OF THE CIVIL WAR, Alexander Gardner. Reproduction of 1866 volume with 100 on-the-field photographs: Manassas, Lincoln on battlefield, slave pens, etc. Introduction by E.F. Bleiler. 224pp. 10¾ x 9.
22731-6 Pa. $5.00

THE MOVIES: A PICTURE QUIZ BOOK, Stanley Appelbaum & Hayward Cirker. Match stars with their movies, name actors and actresses, test your movie skill with 241 stills from 236 great movies, 1902-1959. Indexes of performers and films. 128pp. 8³/8 x 9¼. 20222-4 Pa. $2.50

THE TALKIES, Richard Griffith. Anthology of features, articles from Photoplay, 1928-1940, reproduced complete. Stars, famous movies, technical features, fabulous ads, etc.; Garbo, Chaplin, King Kong, Lubitsch, etc. 4 color plates, scores of illustrations. 327pp. 8³/8 x 11¼. 22762-6 Pa. $6.95

THE MOVIE MUSICAL FROM VITAPHONE TO "42ND STREET," edited by Miles Kreuger. Relive the rise of the movie musical as reported in the pages of Photoplay magazine (1926-1933): every movie review, cast list, ad, and record review; every significant feature article, production still, biography, forecast, and gossip story. Profusely illustrated. 367pp. 8³/8 x 11¼. 23154-2 Pa. $7.95

JOHANN SEBASTIAN BACH, Philipp Spitta. Great classic of biography, musical commentary, with hundreds of pieces analyzed. Also good for Bach's contemporaries. 450 musical examples. Total of 1799pp.
EUK 22278-0, 22279-9 Clothbd., Two vol. set $25.00

BEETHOVEN AND HIS NINE SYMPHONIES, Sir George Grove. Thorough history, analysis, commentary on symphonies and some related pieces. For either beginner or advanced student. 436 musical passages. 407pp. 20334-4 Pa. $4.00

MOZART AND HIS PIANO CONCERTOS, Cuthbert Girdlestone. The only full-length study. Detailed analyses of all 21 concertos, sources; 417 musical examples. 509pp. 21271-8 Pa. $6.00

THE FITZWILLIAM VIRGINAL BOOK, edited by J. Fuller Maitland, W.B. Squire. Famous early 17th century collection of keyboard music, 300 works by Morley, Byrd, Bull, Gibbons, etc. Modern notation. Total of 938pp. 8⅜ x 11.

ECE 21068-5, 21069-3 Pa., Two vol. set $15.00

COMPLETE STRING QUARTETS, Wolfgang A. Mozart. Breitkopf and Härtel edition. All 23 string quartets plus alternate slow movement to K156. Study score. 277pp. 9⅜ x 12¼. 22372-8 Pa. $6.00

COMPLETE SONG CYCLES, Franz Schubert. Complete piano, vocal music of Die Schöne Müllerin, Die Winterreise, Schwanengesang. Also Drinker English singing translations. Breitkopf and Härtel edition. 217pp. 9⅜ x 12¼.

22649-2 Pa. $4.50

THE COMPLETE PRELUDES AND ETUDES FOR PIANOFORTE SOLO, Alexander Scriabin. All the preludes and etudes including many perfectly spun miniatures. Edited by K.N. Igumnov and Y.I. Mil'shteyn. 250pp. 9 x 12. 22919-X Pa. $5.00

TRISTAN UND ISOLDE, Richard Wagner. Full orchestral score with complete instrumentation. Do not confuse with piano reduction. Commentary by Felix Mottl, great Wagnerian conductor and scholar. Study score. 655pp. 8⅛ x 11.

22915-7 Pa. $11.95

FAVORITE SONGS OF THE NINETIES, ed. Robert Fremont. Full reproduction, including covers, of 88 favorites: Ta-Ra-Ra-Boom-De-Aye, The Band Played On, Bird in a Gilded Cage, Under the Bamboo Tree, After the Ball, etc. 401pp. 9 x 12.

EBE 21536-9 Pa. $6.95

SOUSA'S GREAT MARCHES IN PIANO TRANSCRIPTION: ORIGINAL SHEET MUSIC OF 23 WORKS, John Philip Sousa. Selected by Lester S. Levy. Playing edition includes: The Stars and Stripes Forever, The Thunderer, The Gladiator, King Cotton, Washington Post, much more. 24 illustrations. 111pp. 9 x 12.

USO 23132-1 Pa. $3.50

CLASSIC PIANO RAGS, selected with an introduction by Rudi Blesh. Best ragtime music (1897-1922) by Scott Joplin, James Scott, Joseph F. Lamb, Tom Turpin, 9 others. Printed from best original sheet music, plus covers. 364pp. 9 x 12.

EBE 20469-3 Pa. $6.95

ANALYSIS OF CHINESE CHARACTERS, C.D. Wilder, J.H. Ingram. 1000 most important characters analyzed according to primitives, phonetics, historical development. Traditional method offers mnemonic aid to beginner, intermediate student of Chinese, Japanese. 365pp. 23045-7 Pa. $4.00

MODERN CHINESE: A BASIC COURSE, Faculty of Peking University. Self study, classroom course in modern Mandarin. Records contain phonetics, vocabulary, sentences, lessons. 249 page book contains all recorded text, translations, grammar, vocabulary, exercises. Best course on market. 3 12" 33⅓ monaural records, book, album. 98832-5 Set $12.50

THE BEST DR. THORNDYKE DETECTIVE STORIES, R. Austin Freeman. The Case of Oscar Brodski, The Moabite Cipher, and 5 other favorites featuring the great scientific detective, plus his long-believed-lost first adventure — 31 New Inn — reprinted here for the first time. Edited by E.F. Bleiler. USO 20388-3 Pa. $3.00

BEST "THINKING MACHINE" DETECTIVE STORIES, Jacques Futrelle. The Problem of Cell 13 and 11 other stories about Prof. Augustus S.F.X. Van Dusen, including two "lost" stories. First reprinting of several. Edited by E.F. Bleiler. 241pp. 20537-1 Pa. $3.00

UNCLE SILAS, J. Sheridan LeFanu. Victorian Gothic mystery novel, considered by many best of period, even better than Collins or Dickens. Wonderful psychological terror. Introduction by Frederick Shroyer. 436pp. 21715-9 Pa. $4.00

BEST DR. POGGIOLI DETECTIVE STORIES, T.S. Stribling. 15 best stories from EQMM and The Saint offer new adventures in Mexico, Florida, Tennessee hills as Poggioli unravels mysteries and combats Count Jalacki. 217pp. 23227-1 Pa. $3.00

EIGHT DIME NOVELS, selected with an introduction by E.F. Bleiler. Adventures of Old King Brady, Frank James, Nick Carter, Deadwood Dick, Buffalo Bill, The Steam Man, Frank Merriwell, and Horatio Alger — 1877 to 1905. Important, entertaining popular literature in facsimile reprint, with original covers. 190pp. 9 x 12. 22975-0 Pa. $3.50

ALICE'S ADVENTURES UNDER GROUND, Lewis Carroll. Facsimile of ms. Carroll gave Alice Liddell in 1864. Different in many ways from final Alice. Handlettered, illustrated by Carroll. Introduction by Martin Gardner. 128pp. 21482-6 Pa. $1.50

ALICE IN WONDERLAND COLORING BOOK, Lewis Carroll. Pictures by John Tenniel. Large-size versions of the famous illustrations of Alice, Cheshire Cat, Mad Hatter and all the others, waiting for your crayons. Abridged text. 36 illustrations. 64pp. 8¼ x 11. 22853-3 Pa. $1.50

AVENTURES D'ALICE AU PAYS DES MERVEILLES, Lewis Carroll. Bué's translation of "Alice" into French, supervised by Carroll himself. Novel way to learn language. (No English text.) 42 Tenniel illustrations. 196pp. 22836-3 Pa. $2.50

MYTHS AND FOLK TALES OF IRELAND, Jeremiah Curtin. 11 stories that are Irish versions of European fairy tales and 9 stories from the Fenian cycle — 20 tales of legend and magic that comprise an essential work in the history of folklore. 256pp. 22430-9 Pa. $3.00

EAST O' THE SUN AND WEST O' THE MOON, George W. Dasent. Only full edition of favorite, wonderful Norwegian fairytales — Why the Sea is Salt, Boots and the Troll, etc. — with 77 illustrations by Kittelsen & Werenskiöld. 418pp. 22521-6 Pa. $4.00

PERRAULT'S FAIRY TALES, Charles Perrault and Gustave Doré. Original versions of Cinderella, Sleeping Beauty, Little Red Riding Hood, etc. in best translation, with 34 wonderful illustrations by Gustave Doré. 117pp. 8⅛ x 11. 22311-6 Pa. $2.50

MOTHER GOOSE'S MELODIES. Facsimile of fabulously rare Munroe and Francis "copyright 1833" Boston edition. Familiar and unusual rhymes, wonderful old woodcut illustrations. Edited by E.F. Bleiler. 128pp. 4½ x 6⅜. 22577-1 Pa. $1.50

MOTHER GOOSE IN HIEROGLYPHICS. Favorite nursery rhymes presented in rebus form for children. Fascinating 1849 edition reproduced in toto, with key. Introduction by E.F. Bleiler. About 400 woodcuts. 64pp. 6⅞ x 5¼. 20745-5 Pa. $1.00

PETER PIPER'S PRACTICAL PRINCIPLES OF PLAIN & PERFECT PRONUNCIATION. Alliterative jingles and tongue-twisters. Reproduction in full of 1830 first American edition. 25 spirited woodcuts. 32pp. 4½ x 6⅜. 22560-7 Pa. $1.00

MARMADUKE MULTIPLY'S MERRY METHOD OF MAKING MINOR MATHEMATICIANS. Fellow to Peter Piper, it teaches multiplication table by catchy rhymes and woodcuts. 1841 Munroe & Francis edition. Edited by E.F. Bleiler. 4⅝ x 6.
22773-1 Pa. $1.25
20171-6 Clothbd. $3.00

THE NIGHT BEFORE CHRISTMAS, Clement Moore. Full text, and woodcuts from original 1848 book. Also critical, historical material. 19 illustrations. 40pp. 4⅝ x 6. 22797-9 Pa. $1.25

THE KING OF THE GOLDEN RIVER, John Ruskin. Victorian children's classic of three brothers, their attempts to reach the Golden River, what becomes of them. Facsimile of original 1889 edition. 22 illustrations. 56pp. 4⅝ x 6⅜.
20066-3 Pa. $1.50

DREAMS OF THE RAREBIT FIEND, Winsor McCay. Pioneer cartoon strip, unexcelled for beauty, imagination, in 60 full sequences. Incredible technical virtuosity, wonderful visual wit. Historical introduction. 62pp. 8⅜ x 11¼. 21347-1 Pa. $2.50

THE KATZENJAMMER KIDS, Rudolf Dirks. In full color, 14 strips from 1906-7; full of imagination, characteristic humor. Classic of great historical importance. Introduction by August Derleth. 32pp. 9¼ x 12¼. 23005-8 Pa. $2.00

LITTLE ORPHAN ANNIE AND LITTLE ORPHAN ANNIE IN COSMIC CITY, Harold Gray. Two great sequences from the early strips: our curly-haired heroine defends the Warbucks' financial empire and, then, takes on meanie Phineas P. Pinchpenny. Leapin' lizards! 178pp. 6⅛ x 8⅜. 23107-0 Pa. $2.00

THE BEST OF GLUYAS WILLIAMS. 100 drawings by one of America's finest cartoonists: The Day a Cake of Ivory Soap Sank at Proctor & Gamble's, At the Life Insurance Agents' Banquet, and many other gems from the 20's and 30's. 118pp. 8⅜ x 11¼. 22737-5 Pa. $2.50

THE MAGIC MOVING PICTURE BOOK, Bliss, Sands & Co. The pictures in this book move! Volcanoes erupt, a house burns, a serpentine dancer wiggles her way through a number. By using a specially ruled acetate screen provided, you can obtain these and 15 other startling effects. Originally "The Motograph Moving Picture Book." 32pp. 8¼ x 11. 23224-7 Pa. $1.75

STRING FIGURES AND HOW TO MAKE THEM, Caroline F. Jayne. Fullest, clearest instructions on string figures from around world: Eskimo, Navajo, Lapp, Europe, more. Cats cradle, moving spear, lightning, stars. Introduction by A.C. Haddon. 950 illustrations. 407pp. 20152-X Pa. $3.50

PAPER FOLDING FOR BEGINNERS, William D. Murray and Francis J. Rigney. Clearest book on market for making origami sail boats, roosters, frogs that move legs, cups, bonbon boxes. 40 projects. More than 275 illustrations. Photographs. 94pp. 20713-7 Pa. $1.25

INDIAN SIGN LANGUAGE, William Tomkins. Over 525 signs developed by Sioux, Blackfoot, Cheyenne, Arapahoe and other tribes. Written instructions and diagrams: how to make words, construct sentences. Also 290 pictographs of Sioux and Ojibway tribes. 111pp. 6⅛ x 9¼. 22029-X Pa. $1.50

BOOMERANGS: HOW TO MAKE AND THROW THEM, Bernard S. Mason. Easy to make and throw, dozens of designs: cross-stick, pinwheel, boomabird, tumblestick, Australian curved stick boomerang. Complete throwing instructions. All safe. 99pp. 23028-7 Pa. $1.75

25 KITES THAT FLY, Leslie Hunt. Full, easy to follow instructions for kites made from inexpensive materials. Many novelties. Reeling, raising, designing your own. 70 illustrations. 110pp. 22550-X Pa. $1.25

TRICKS AND GAMES ON THE POOL TABLE, Fred Herrmann. 79 tricks and games, some solitaires, some for 2 or more players, some competitive; mystifying shots and throws, unusual carom, tricks involving cork, coins, a hat, more. 77 figures. 95pp. 21814-7 Pa. $1.25

WOODCRAFT AND CAMPING, Bernard S. Mason. How to make a quick emergency shelter, select woods that will burn immediately, make do with limited supplies, etc. Also making many things out of wood, rawhide, bark, at camp. Formerly titled Woodcraft. 295 illustrations. 580pp. 21951-8 Pa. $4.00

AN INTRODUCTION TO CHESS MOVES AND TACTICS SIMPLY EXPLAINED, Leonard Barden. Informal intermediate introduction: reasons for moves, tactics, openings, traps, positional play, endgame. Isolates patterns. 102pp. USO 21210-6 Pa. $1.35

LASKER'S MANUAL OF CHESS, Dr. Emanuel Lasker. Great world champion offers very thorough coverage of all aspects of chess. Combinations, position play, openings, endgame, aesthetics of chess, philosophy of struggle, much more. Filled with analyzed games. 390pp. 20640-8 Pa. $4.00

CATALOGUE OF DOVER BOOKS

DRIED FLOWERS, Sarah Whitlock and Martha Rankin. Concise, clear, practical guide to dehydration, glycerinizing, pressing plant material, and more. Covers use of silica gel. 12 drawings. Originally titled "New Techniques with Dried Flowers." 32pp. 21802-3 Pa. $1.00

ABC OF POULTRY RAISING, J.H. Florea. Poultry expert, editor tells how to raise chickens on home or small business basis. Breeds, feeding, housing, laying, etc. Very concrete, practical. 50 illustrations. 256pp. 23201-8 Pa. $3.00

HOW INDIANS USE WILD PLANTS FOR FOOD, MEDICINE & CRAFTS, Frances Densmore. Smithsonian, Bureau of American Ethnology report presents wealth of material on nearly 200 plants used by Chippewas of Minnesota and Wisconsin. 33 plates plus 122pp. of text. 6⅛ x 9¼. 23019-8 Pa. $2.50

THE HERBAL OR GENERAL HISTORY OF PLANTS, John Gerard. The 1633 edition revised and enlarged by Thomas Johnson. Containing almost 2850 plant descriptions and 2705 superb illustrations, Gerard's Herbal is a monumental work, the book all modern English herbals are derived from, and the one herbal every serious enthusiast should have in its entirety. Original editions are worth perhaps $750. 1678pp. 8½ x 12¼. 23147-X Clothbd. $50.00

A MODERN HERBAL, Margaret Grieve. Much the fullest, most exact, most useful compilation of herbal material. Gigantic alphabetical encyclopedia, from aconite to zedoary, gives botanical information, medical properties, folklore, economic uses, and much else. Indispensable to serious reader. 161 illustrations. 888pp. 6½ x 9¼. USO 22798-7, 22799-5 Pa., Two vol. set $10.00

HOW TO KNOW THE FERNS, Frances T. Parsons. Delightful classic. Identification, fern lore, for Eastern and Central U.S.A. Has introduced thousands to interesting life form. 99 illustrations. 215pp. 20740-4 Pa. $2.75

THE MUSHROOM HANDBOOK, Louis C.C. Krieger. Still the best popular handbook. Full descriptions of 259 species, extremely thorough text, habitats, luminescence, poisons, folklore, etc. 32 color plates; 126 other illustrations. 560pp. 21861-9 Pa. $4.50

HOW TO KNOW THE WILD FRUITS, Maude G. Peterson. Classic guide covers nearly 200 trees, shrubs, smaller plants of the U.S. arranged by color of fruit and then by family. Full text provides names, descriptions, edibility, uses. 80 illustrations. 400pp. 22943-2 Pa. $4.00

COMMON WEEDS OF THE UNITED STATES, U.S. Department of Agriculture. Covers 220 important weeds with illustration, maps, botanical information, plant lore for each. Over 225 illustrations. 463pp. 6⅛ x 9¼. 20504-5 Pa. $4.50

HOW TO KNOW THE WILD FLOWERS, Mrs. William S. Dana. Still best popular book for East and Central USA. Over 500 plants easily identified, with plant lore; arranged according to color and flowering time. 174 plates. 459pp. 20332-8 Pa. $3.50

DRIED FLOWERS, Sarah Whitlock and Martha Rankin. Concise, clear, practical guide to dehydration, glycerinizing, pressing plant material, and more. Covers use of silica gel. 12 drawings. Originally titled "New Techniques with Dried Flowers." 32pp. 21802-3 Pa. $1.00

ABC OF POULTRY RAISING, J.H. Florea. Poultry expert, editor tells how to raise chickens on home or small business basis. Breeds, feeding, housing, laying, etc. Very concrete, practical. 50 illustrations. 256pp. 23201-8 Pa. $3.00

HOW INDIANS USE WILD PLANTS FOR FOOD, MEDICINE & CRAFTS, Frances Densmore. Smithsonian, Bureau of American Ethnology report presents wealth of material on nearly 200 plants used by Chippewas of Minnesota and Wisconsin. 33 plates plus 122pp. of text. 6⅛ x 9¼. 23019-8 Pa. $2.50

THE HERBAL OR GENERAL HISTORY OF PLANTS, John Gerard. The 1633 edition revised and enlarged by Thomas Johnson. Containing almost 2850 plant descriptions and 2705 superb illustrations, Gerard's Herbal is a monumental work, the book all modern English herbals are derived from, and the one herbal every serious enthusiast should have in its entirety. Original editions are worth perhaps $750. 1678pp. 8½ x 12¼. 23147-X Clothbd. $50.00

A MODERN HERBAL, Margaret Grieve. Much the fullest, most exact, most useful compilation of herbal material. Gigantic alphabetical encyclopedia, from aconite to zedoary, gives botanical information, medical properties, folklore, economic uses, and much else. Indispensable to serious reader. 161 illustrations. 888pp. 6½ x 9¼. USO 22798-7, 22799-5 Pa., Two vol. set $10.00

HOW TO KNOW THE FERNS, Frances T. Parsons. Delightful classic. Identification, fern lore, for Eastern and Central U.S.A. Has introduced thousands to interesting life form. 99 illustrations. 215pp. 20740-4 Pa. $2.75

THE MUSHROOM HANDBOOK, Louis C.C. Krieger. Still the best popular handbook. Full descriptions of 259 species, extremely thorough text, habitats, luminescence, poisons, folklore, etc. 32 color plates; 126 other illustrations. 560pp. 21861-9 Pa. $4.50

HOW TO KNOW THE WILD FRUITS, Maude G. Peterson. Classic guide covers nearly 200 trees, shrubs, smaller plants of the U.S. arranged by color of fruit and then by family. Full text provides names, descriptions, edibility, uses. 80 illustrations. 400pp. 22943-2 Pa. $4.00

COMMON WEEDS OF THE UNITED STATES, U.S. Department of Agriculture. Covers 220 important weeds with illustration, maps, botanical information, plant lore for each. Over 225 illustrations. 463pp. 6⅛ x 9¼. 20504-5 Pa. $4.50

HOW TO KNOW THE WILD FLOWERS, Mrs. William S. Dana. Still best popular book for East and Central USA. Over 500 plants easily identified, with plant lore; arranged according to color and flowering time. 174 plates. 459pp. 20332-8 Pa. $3.50

THE STYLE OF PALESTRINA AND THE DISSONANCE, Knud Jeppesen. Standard analysis of rhythm, line, harmony, accented and unaccented dissonances. Also pre-Palestrina dissonances. 306pp. 22386-8 Pa. $4.50

DOVER OPERA GUIDE AND LIBRETTO SERIES prepared by Ellen H. Bleiler. Each volume contains everything needed for background, complete enjoyment: complete libretto, new English translation with all repeats, biography of composer and librettist, early performance history, musical lore, much else. All volumes lavishly illustrated with performance photos, portraits, similar material. Do not confuse with skimpy performance booklets.

CARMEN, Georges Bizet. 66 illustrations. 222pp. 22111-3 Pa. $3.00
DON GIOVANNI, Wolfgang A. Mozart. 92 illustrations. 209pp. 21134-7 Pa. $2.50
LA BOHÈME, Giacomo Puccini. 73 illustrations. 124pp. USO 20404-9 Pa. $1.75
ÄIDA, Giuseppe Verdi. 76 illustrations. 181pp. 20405-7 Pa. $2.25
LUCIA DI LAMMERMOOR, Gaetano Donizetti. 44 illustrations. 186pp. 22110-5 Pa. $2.00

ANTONIO STRADIVARI: HIS LIFE AND WORK, W. H. Hill, et al. Great work of musicology. Construction methods, woods, varnishes, known instruments, types of instruments, life, special features. Introduction by Sydney Beck. 98 illustrations, plus 4 color plates. 315pp. 20425-1 Pa. $4.00

MUSIC FOR THE PIANO, James Friskin, Irwin Freundlich. Both famous, little-known compositions; 1500 to 1950's. Listing, description, classification, technical aspects for student, teacher, performer. Indispensable for enlarging repertory. 448pp. 22918-1 Pa. $4.00

PIANOS AND THEIR MAKERS, Alfred Dolge. Leading inventor offers full history of piano technology, earliest models to 1910. Types, makers, components, mechanisms, musical aspects. Very strong on offtrail models, inventions; also player pianos. 300 illustrations. 581pp. 22856-8 Pa. $5.00

KEYBOARD MUSIC, J.S. Bach. Bach-Gesellschaft edition. For harpsichord, piano, other keyboard instruments. English Suites, French Suites, Six Partitas, Goldberg Variations, Two-Part Inventions, Three-Part Sinfonias. 312pp. 8⅛ x 11. 22360-4 Pa. $5.00

COMPLETE STRING QUARTETS, Ludwig van Beethoven. Breitkopf and Härtel edition. 6 quartets of Opus 18; 3 quartets of Opus 59; Opera 74, 95, 127, 130, 131, 132, 135 and Grosse Fuge. Study score. 434pp. 9⅜ x 12¼. 22361-2 Pa. $7.95

COMPLETE PIANO SONATAS AND VARIATIONS FOR SOLO PIANO, Johannes Brahms. All sonatas, five variations on themes from Schumann, Paganini, Handel, etc. Vienna Gesellschaft der Musikfreunde edition. 178pp. 9 x 12. 22650-6 Pa. $4.50

PIANO MUSIC 1888-1905, Claude Debussy. Deux Arabesques, Suite Bergamesque, Masques, 1st series of Images, etc. 9 others, in corrected editions. 175pp. 9⅜ x 12¼. 22771-5 Pa. $4.00

INCIDENTS OF TRAVEL IN YUCATAN, John L. Stephens. Classic (1843) exploration of jungles of Yucatan, looking for evidences of Maya civilization. Travel adventures, Mexican and Indian culture, etc. Total of 669pp.
20926-1, 20927-X Pa., Two vol. set $6.00

LIVING MY LIFE, Emma Goldman. Candid, no holds barred account by foremost American anarchist: her own life, anarchist movement, famous contemporaries, ideas and their impact. Struggles and confrontations in America, plus deportation to U.S.S.R. Shocking inside account of persecution of anarchists under Lenin. 13 plates. Total of 944pp.
22543-7, 22544-5 Pa., Two vol. set $9.00

AMERICAN INDIANS, George Catlin. Classic account of life among Plains Indians: ceremonies, hunt, warfare, etc. Dover edition reproduces for first time all original paintings. 312 plates. 572pp. of text. 6⅛ x 9¼.
22118-0, 22119-9 Pa., Two vol. set $8.00
22140-7, 22144-X Clothbd., Two vol. set $16.00

THE INDIANS BOOK, Natalie Curtis. Lore, music, narratives, drawings by Indians, collected from cultures of U.S.A. 149 songs in full notation. 45 illustrations. 583pp. 6⅝ x 9⅜.
21939-9 Pa. $6.95

INDIAN BLANKETS AND THEIR MAKERS, George Wharton James. History, old style wool blankets, changes brought about by traders, symbolism of design and color, a Navajo weaver at work, outline blanket, Kachina blankets, more. Emphasis on Navajo. 130 illustrations, 32 in color. 230pp. 6⅛ x 9¼.
22996-3 Pa. $5.00
23068-6 Clothbd. $10.00

AN INTRODUCTION TO THE STUDY OF THE MAYA HIEROGLYPHS, Sylvanus Griswold Morley. Classic study by one of the truly great figures in hieroglyph research. Still the best introduction for the student for reading Maya hieroglyphs. New introduction by J. Eric S. Thompson. 117 illustrations. 284pp.
23108-9 Pa. $4.00

THE ANALECTS OF CONFUCIUS, THE GREAT LEARNING, DOCTRINE OF THE MEAN, Confucius. Edited by James Legge. Full Chinese text, standard English translation on same page, Chinese commentators, editor's annotations; dictionary of characters at rear, plus grammatical comment. Finest edition anywhere of one of world's greatest thinkers. 503pp.
22746-4 Pa. $5.00

THE I CHING (THE BOOK OF CHANGES), translated by James Legge. Complete translation of basic text plus appendices by Confucius, and Chinese commentary of most penetrating divination manual ever prepared. Indispensable to study of early Oriental civilizations, to modern inquiring reader. 448pp.
21062-6 Pa. $3.50

THE EGYPTIAN BOOK OF THE DEAD, E.A. Wallis Budge. Complete reproduction of Ani's papyrus, finest ever found. Full hieroglyphic text, interlinear transliteration, word for word translation, smooth translation. Basic work, for Egyptology, for modern study of psychic matters. Total of 533pp. 6½ x 9¼.
EBE 21866-X Pa. $4.95

BUILD YOUR OWN LOW-COST HOME, L.O. Anderson, H.F. Zornig. U.S. Dept. of Agriculture sets of plans, full, detailed, for 11 houses: A-Frame, circular, conventional. Also construction manual. Save hundreds of dollars. 204pp. 11 x 16.
21525-3 Pa. $6.00

HOW TO BUILD A WOOD-FRAME HOUSE, L.O. Anderson. Comprehensive, easy to follow U.S. Government manual: placement, foundations, framing, sheathing, roof, insulation, plaster, finishing — almost everything else. 179 illustrations. 223pp. 7⅞ x 10¾.
22954-8 Pa. $3.50

CONCRETE, MASONRY AND BRICKWORK, U.S. Department of the Army. Practical handbook for the home owner and small builder, manual contains basic principles, techniques, and important background information on construction with concrete, concrete blocks, and brick. 177 figures, 37 tables. 200pp. 6½ x 9¼.
23203-4 Pa. $4.00

THE STANDARD BOOK OF QUILT MAKING AND COLLECTING, Marguerite Ickis. Full information, full-sized patterns for making 46 traditional quilts, also 150 other patterns. Quilted cloths, lamé, satin quilts, etc. 483 illustrations. 273pp. 6⅞ x 9⅝.
20582-7 Pa. $3.50

101 PATCHWORK PATTERNS, Ruby S. McKim. 101 beautiful, immediately useable patterns, full-size, modern and traditional. Also general information, estimating, quilt lore. 124pp. 7⅞ x 10¾.
20773-0 Pa. $2.50

KNIT YOUR OWN NORWEGIAN SWEATERS, Dale Yarn Company. Complete instructions for 50 authentic sweaters, hats, mittens, gloves, caps, etc. Thoroughly modern designs that command high prices in stores. 24 patterns, 24 color photographs. Nearly 100 charts and other illustrations. 58pp. 8⅜ x 11¼.
23031-7 Pa. $2.50

IRON-ON TRANSFER PATTERNS FOR CREWEL AND EMBROIDERY FROM EARLY AMERICAN SOURCES, edited by Rita Weiss. 75 designs, borders, alphabets, from traditional American sources printed on translucent paper in transfer ink. Reuseable. Instructions. Test patterns. 24pp. 8¼ x 11.
23162-3 Pa. $1.50

AMERICAN INDIAN NEEDLEPOINT DESIGNS FOR PILLOWS, BELTS, HANDBAGS AND OTHER PROJECTS, Roslyn Epstein. 37 authentic American Indian designs adapted for modern needlepoint projects. Grid backing makes designs easily transferable to canvas. 48pp. 8¼ x 11.
22973-4 Pa. $1.50

CHARTED FOLK DESIGNS FOR CROSS-STITCH EMBROIDERY, Maria Foris & Andreas Foris. 278 charted folk designs, most in 2 colors, from Danube region: florals, fantastic beasts, geometrics, traditional symbols, more. Border and central patterns. 77pp. 8¼ x 11.
USO 23191-7 Pa. $2.00

Prices subject to change without notice.
Available at your book dealer or write for free catalogue to Dept. GI, Dover Publications, Inc., 180 Varick St., N.Y., N.Y. 10014. Dover publishes more than 150 books each year on science, elementary and advanced mathematics, biology, music, art, literary history, social sciences and other areas.